محمد

AN-NAWAWI'S 40 HADITH

الاربعون النووية

Arabic Text - Translation - Summarised Lessons

DCB RESEARCH

Published by

Dakwah Corner Bookstore (M) Sdn. Bhd
No. 7, Jalan Dato Abdul Aziz, Section 14
46100 Petaling Jaya, Selangor Darul Ehsan
MALAYSIA
T: +603-7956 466

Year of Publication:
2020

Title:
An-Nawawi's 40 Hadith

Author:
DCB Research

ISBN:
978-967-1256-56-5

Director:
Farid Ullah Ahmed Hussain

Cover Design:
Mohammed Faraz

Typesetting:
Every Edition Sdn. Bhd.

Printed by:
Percetakan Azman Sdn. Bhd.

For suggestions and comments:
dakwahcornerpublications@gmail.com

Showroom Outlets

MALAYSIA

Dakwah Corner Bookstore
Ampang Point Shopping Centre
Tel: +60 3 4266 9692

Dakwah Corner Bookstore
G15 (Ground Floor)
Amcorp Mall,
Petaling Jaya

SAUDI ARABIA

Dawah Corner Bookstore
Makkah Commercial Center, Holy Makkah
Tel: +966 125311 895

NIGERIA

Dawah Islamic Bookshop
UAC Building,
Abuja
Tel: +234 805 603 7779

Distributors

Darussalam Australia
Australia
Tel: +61 2 9740 7188

Salaam Media International
Singapore
Tel: +65 63964121

Darussalam Publishers
USA
Tel: +1 860 224 2400

Darussalam Books (London Central Mosque),
UK
Tel: +44 2077231234

CONTENTS

HADITH	TITLE / *Page*

Foreword

بسم الله الرحمن الرحيم

In the Name of Allāh The Most Gracious and The Most Merciful

The collection of forty *ḥadīths* by Imam al-Nawawī has been known, accepted, and appreciated by Muslim scholars for the last seven centuries. Its significance lay in the fact that these selected forty *ḥadīths* comprise the essential fundamental concepts of Islam, which in turn construct the minimum level of required revealed knowledge for every single Muslim. Most of them are authentic *ḥadīths* collected from al-Bukhārī and Muslim.

In fact, Imam al-Nawawī had a very short life of 44 years, but even during this short period he wrote a large number of books on various subjects. Nearly every work is a masterpiece and a treasure of knowledge. Hundreds of thousands of people have benefited from these works.

Among the prestigious works of Imam al-Nawawī is the compilation of the *Forty Ḥadīth* which is what you have in your hands right now.

Dakwah Corner Publications is pleased to deliver to you this great Imam's work in a new look – valued as a modern presentation with selected summarized lessons for each *ḥadīth* based on the famous commentaries by Imam Ibn Daqīq, Dr. Jamaluddin Zarabozo, and Dr. Jamal Badi.

We ask Allāh the Almighty to accept this work from us and make it beneficial for others, *āmīn*.

Farid Ullah bin Ahmed Hussain

الحديث الأول

First Ḥadīth

Actions are Judged by Intentions

عَنْ أَمِيرِ الْمُؤْمِنِينَ أَبِي حَفْصٍ عُمَرَ بْنِ الْخَطَّابِ رضي الله عنه قَالَ: سَمِعْتُ رَسُولَ اللهِ ﷺ يَقُولُ «إِنَّمَا الْأَعْمَالُ بِالنِّيَّاتِ، وَإِنَّمَا لِكُلِّ امْرِئٍ مَا نَوَى، فَمَنْ كَانَتْ هِجْرَتُهُ إِلَى اللهِ وَرَسُولِهِ فَهِجْرَتُهُ إِلَى اللهِ وَرَسُولِهِ، وَمَنْ كَانَتْ هِجْرَتُهُ لِدُنْيَا يُصِيبُهَا أَوْ امْرَأَةٍ يَنْكِحُهَا فَهِجْرَتُهُ إِلَى مَا هَاجَرَ إِلَيْهِ.»

رَوَاهُ الْبُخَارِيُّ [رقم ١] وَمُسْلِمٌ [رقم ٣٦٤١].

It is narrated on the authority of Amīr al-Mu'minīn Abū Ḥafṣ 'Umar bin al-Khaṭṭāb رضي الله عنه, who said, "I heard the Messenger of Allāh صلى الله عليه وسلم say, «Actions are judged by *niyyāt* (intentions), so each man will have what he intended. Thus, he whose *hijrah* (migration) is for Allāh and His Messenger, his migration is for Allāh and His Messenger; but he whose migration is for some worldly thing he might gain, or for a wife he may marry, his migration is for that which he migrated for.»"

Al-Bukhārī and *Muslim*.

Summarised Lessons

- Every conscious, *free-willed* act has an intention behind it that is driving it and bringing it about.
- A person will achieve whatever he intended. If he intended good, good will come about. If he intended evil, evil will come about—that is, the result will be evil for him.
- If a person does a proper deed solely for the sake of Allāh, his purpose would have been met and the deed would be accepted by Allāh.
- Even such noble deeds as emigrating that should be done for the sake of Allāh may be performed with a less noble intention. In such cases, the person will only get what he intended.
- This world and the opposite sex in particular are two aspects that drive a

person to perform certain deeds. They can have great influences over a person, to the extent that one may even perform noble deeds not for the sake of Allāh but for their sake.

الحديث الثاني

Second Ḥadīth

Islam, *Īmān*, and *Iḥsān*

عَنْ عُمَرَ رَضِيَ اللهُ عَنْهُ أَيْضًا قَالَ: بَيْنَمَا نَحْنُ جُلُوسٌ عِنْدَ رَسُولِ اللهِ ﷺ ذَاتَ يَوْمٍ، إِذْ طَلَعَ عَلَيْنَا رَجُلٌ شَدِيدُ بَيَاضِ الثِّيَابِ، شَدِيدُ سَوَادِ الشَّعْرِ، لَا يُرَى عَلَيْهِ أَثَرُ السَّفَرِ، وَلَا يَعْرِفُهُ مِنَّا أَحَدٌ. حَتَّى جَلَسَ إِلَى النَّبِيِّ ﷺ. فَأَسْنَدَ رُكْبَتَيْهِ إِلَى رُكْبَتَيْهِ، وَوَضَعَ كَفَّيْهِ عَلَى فَخِذَيْهِ، وَقَالَ: يَا مُحَمَّدُ أَخْبِرْنِي عَنِ الْإِسْلَامِ. فَقَالَ رَسُولُ اللهِ ﷺ «الْإِسْلَامُ أَنْ تَشْهَدَ أَنْ لَا إِلَهَ إِلَّا اللهُ وَأَنَّ مُحَمَّدًا رَسُولُ اللهِ، وَتُقِيمَ الصَّلَاةَ، وَتُؤْتِيَ الزَّكَاةَ، وَتَصُومَ رَمَضَانَ، وَتَحُجَّ الْبَيْتَ إِنْ اسْتَطَعْتَ إِلَيْهِ سَبِيلًا.» قَالَ: صَدَقْتَ. فَعَجِبْنَا لَهُ يَسْأَلُهُ وَيُصَدِّقُهُ!

قَالَ: فَأَخْبِرْنِي عَنِ الْإِيمَانِ. قَالَ «أَنْ تُؤْمِنَ بِاللهِ وَمَلَائِكَتِهِ وَكُتُبِهِ وَرُسُلِهِ وَالْيَوْمِ الْآخِرِ، وَتُؤْمِنَ بِالْقَدَرِ

خَيْرِهِ وَشَرِّهِ.» قَالَ: صَدَقْت. قَالَ: فَأَخْبِرْنِي عَنْ الْإِحْسَانِ. قَالَ «أَنْ تَعْبُدَ اللَّهَ كَأَنَّك تَرَاهُ، فَإِنْ لَمْ تَكُنْ تَرَاهُ فَإِنَّهُ يَرَاك.»

قَالَ: فَأَخْبِرْنِي عَنْ السَّاعَةِ. قَالَ «مَا الْمَسْئُولُ عَنْهَا بِأَعْلَمَ مِنْ السَّائِلِ.» قَالَ: فَأَخْبِرْنِي عَنْ أَمَارَاتِهَا؟ قَالَ «أَنْ تَلِدَ الْأَمَةُ رَبَّتَهَا، وَأَنْ تَرَى الْحُفَاةَ الْعُرَاةَ الْعَالَةَ رِعَاءَ الشَّاءِ يَتَطَاوَلُونَ فِي الْبُنْيَانِ.» ثُمَّ انْطَلَقَ، فَلَبِثْنَا مَلِيًّا، ثُمَّ قَالَ «يَا عُمَرُ أَتَدْرِي مَنْ السَّائِلُ؟» قُلْتُ: اللَّهُ وَرَسُولُهُ أَعْلَمُ. قَالَ: «فَإِنَّهُ جِبْرِيلُ أَتَاكُمْ يُعَلِّمُكُمْ دِينَكُمْ.»

رَوَاهُ مُسْلِمٌ [رقم ٨].

On the authority of ʿUmar رضي الله عنه, who said, "While we were one day sitting with the Messenger of Allāh صلى الله عليه وسلم there appeared before us a man dressed in extremely white clothes and with extremely black hair. No traces of travel were visible on him, and none of us knew him. He sat down close by the Prophet صلى الله عليه وسلم, rested his knee against his knees, and placed his hands on his thighs, and said, 'O Muḥammad! Inform me about

Islam.' The Messenger of Allāh صَلَّى ٱللَّٰهُ عَلَيْهِ وَسَلَّمَ said, «Islam is that you should testify that there is no deity except Allāh, and that Muḥammad is His Messenger, that you should establish Ṣalāh, pay the Zakāh, fast during Ramaḍān, and perform Ḥajj to the House (Ka'bah) if you find the means for making the journey to it.» He said, 'You have spoken truly.' We were astonished at his thus questioning him صَلَّى ٱللَّٰهُ عَلَيْهِ وَسَلَّمَ and then telling him that he was right.

He went on to say, 'Inform me about Īmān (faith).' He (the Prophet) answered, «It is that you believe in Allāh, His Angels, His Books, His Messengers, the Last Day, and in fate (*qadar*), both in its good and in its evil aspects.» He said, 'You have spoken the truth.' Then he (the man) said, 'Inform me about Iḥsān.' He (the Prophet) answered, «It is that you should serve Allāh as though you could see Him, for though you cannot see Him yet He sees you.»

He said, 'Inform me about the Hour.' He (the Prophet) said, «About that the one questioned knows no more than the questioner.» So he said, 'Well, inform me about its signs.' He (the Prophet) said, «They are that the slave-girl will give birth to her mistress and that you will see the barefooted ones, the naked, the destitute, the herdsmen of sheep (competing with each other) in raising lofty buildings.» Thereupon the man went off. I waited a while, and then he (the Prophet) said, «O ʿUmar, do you know who that questioner was?» I replied, 'Allāh and His Messenger know better.' He said, 'That was Jibril. He came to teach you your religion.'"

Muslim.

Summarised Lessons

- The pillars or foundation upon which Islam rests are five: the declaration of the testimony of faith, the establishment of the prayers, the paying of Zakāt, the fasting of Ramaḍān and the pilgrimage.
- The articles of faith in which all Muslims must believe are six: belief in Allāh, the Angels, the Books, the Messengers, the Day of Resurrection, and Divine Decree.
- As for *ihsān*, al-Nawawī's following statement provides an excellent summary of the Messenger of Allāh's صَلَّى ٱللَّهُ عَلَيْهِ وَسَلَّمَ answer to the meaning of *ihsān*, "This is one of the comprehensive expressions that the Messenger of Allāh صَلَّى ٱللَّهُ عَلَيْهِ وَسَلَّمَ was given. This is because if anyone of us could stand in worship while he is seeing Allāh, then he would not leave anything

that would be in his ability of submission, humility, fear, beautiful features, and combine them all both outwardly and inwardly. One would take care to complete the act in the best possible way...Hence, the purpose of these words is to encourage purity in worship and recognition by the person that his Lord is watching him, so that he will be as complete as possible when it comes to submission, humility, and fear."

- The religion or *dīn* is comprised of the three different levels of Islam, Īmān, and Iḥsān. The one who continues only at the level of Islam until he dies will be saved from being forever in the Hell-fire, although he may enter it due to his sins. On the other hand, the one who continues in *ihsān* until he dies will go directly to Paradise and will have the pleasure of seeing Allāh in the Hereafter.

- The knowledge of when the Hour will be established is known only to Allāh. The noblest of mankind and the noblest of the angels demonstrated that they have no knowledge of when it will occur. Some Shiites and Sufis make outlandish claims that their Imams and saints have knowledge of the Unseen—some even say that the saints look at the Preserved

Tablet. In fact, some even claim that their Imams or saints have all the knowledge, just like Allāh. These beliefs go against the Quran and Sunnah and if a person insists on them even after being shown their falsehood, the insistence on this belief takes him out of the fold of Islam.

- Allāh has blessed mankind with the knowledge of some of the signs of the Hour. These signs that occur around the person should act as reminders of the coming Hour and Judgement. This should also remind him that Allāh sees and knows all things, including what the person himself is doing at any moment.

الحديث الثالث

Third Ḥadīth

The Pillars of Islam

عَنْ أَبِي عَبْدِ الرَّحْمَنِ عَبْدِ اللهِ بْنِ عُمَرَ بْنِ الْخَطَّابِ رضي الله عنهما قَالَ: سَمِعْتُ رَسُولَ اللهِ ﷺ يَقُولُ «بُنِيَ الْإِسْلَامُ عَلَى خَمْسٍ: شَهَادَةِ أَنْ لَا إِلَهَ إِلَّا اللهُ وَأَنَّ مُحَمَّدًا رَسُولُ اللهِ، وَإِقَامِ الصَّلَاةِ، وَإِيتَاءِ الزَّكَاةِ، وَحَجِّ الْبَيْتِ، وَصَوْمِ رَمَضَانَ.»

رَوَاهُ الْبُخَارِيُّ [رقم ٨] وَمُسْلِمٌ [رقم ١٦].

On the authority of Abū ʿAbdir-Raḥmān ʿAbdullāh bin ʿUmar bin al-Khaṭṭāb رَضِيَ اللَّهُ عَنْهُمَا who said, "I heard the Messenger of Allāh صَلَّى اللَّهُ عَلَيْهِ وَسَلَّمَ saying, «Islam has been built upon five things: on testifying that there is no God save Allah, and that Muḥammad is His Messenger; performing Ṣalāh; giving the Zakāh; performance of Ḥajj to the House; and fasting during Ramaḍān.»"

Al-Bukhārī and *Muslim*.

Summarised Lessons

- One can derive the following from the five pillars: Acts of worship are either acts of performance or acts of avoidance. Fasting is from the latter category while the other pillars are from the former. In addition, the acts of worship are acts of the tongue (like the testimony of faith and parts of the prayer), acts of the body (like prayer), acts related to one's wealth (like Zakāt) and acts that are of the body and wealth (like Ḥajj).

- This *ḥadīth* states what Islam is built upon. These are the foundations of one's Islam. If these foundations or pillars are strong, Allāh willing, the rest of one's faith and religion will also be sound, correct and strong. However, if these pillars are weak or not sound, it is not surprising that there may be some problems further on down the line. In fact, one should expect that there will be some problems or weaknesses in the person's submission to Allāh and his faith.

- If anyone denies the obligation of any of the pillars of Islam, he becomes a disbeliever. These pillars are firmly established in this particular *ḥadīth* as well as in numerous verses of the Quran and other *ḥadīth*.

- There is a consensus that if one nullifies the first pillar mentioned by the Prophet صَلَّى ٱللَّهُ عَلَيْهِ وَسَلَّمَ, one negates his Islam and becomes a disbeliever.

- There is a disagreement concerning the second pillar. Many scholars are of the opinion that one who does not pray also leaves the fold of Islam. The majority say that he is an evil doer who deserves to be killed as a punishment for his sin.

- Concerning Zakāt, Ḥajj, and fasting, there is at least one statement from at least one Companion that implies that the person who willingly does not perform any of these acts falls outside of the fold of Islam. Again, the majority opinion is that such people do not become disbelievers although their sins are heinous. In any case, the statements of those Companions should be taken seriously and a Muslim should not take abandoning these actions lightly at all.

الحديث الرابع
Fourth Ḥadīth
The Creation of the Human Being and *Qadr*

عَنْ أَبِي عَبْدِ الرَّحْمَنِ عَبْدِ اللَّهِ بْنِ مَسْعُودٍ رَضِيَ اللَّهُ عَنْهُ قَالَ: حَدَّثَنَا رَسُولُ اللَّهِ ﷺ وَهُوَ الصَّادِقُ الْمَصْدُوقُ «إِنَّ أَحَدَكُمْ يُجْمَعُ خَلْقُهُ فِي بَطْنِ أُمِّهِ أَرْبَعِينَ يَوْمًا نُطْفَةً، ثُمَّ يَكُونُ عَلَقَةً مِثْلَ ذَلِكَ، ثُمَّ يَكُونُ مُضْغَةً مِثْلَ ذَلِكَ، ثُمَّ يُرْسَلُ إِلَيْهِ الْمَلَكُ فَيَنْفُخُ فِيهِ الرُّوحَ، وَيُؤْمَرُ بِأَرْبَعِ كَلِمَاتٍ: بِكَتْبِ رِزْقِهِ، وَأَجَلِهِ، وَعَمَلِهِ، وَشَقِيٌّ أَمْ سَعِيدٌ؛ فَوَاللَّهِ الَّذِي لَا إِلَهَ غَيْرُهُ إِنَّ أَحَدَكُمْ لَيَعْمَلُ بِعَمَلِ أَهْلِ الْجَنَّةِ حَتَّى مَا يَكُونُ بَيْنَهُ وَبَيْنَهَا إِلَّا ذِرَاعٌ فَيَسْبِقُ عَلَيْهِ الْكِتَابُ فَيَعْمَلُ بِعَمَلِ أَهْلِ النَّارِ فَيَدْخُلُهَا. وَإِنَّ أَحَدَكُمْ لَيَعْمَلُ بِعَمَلِ أَهْلِ النَّارِ

حَتَّى مَا يَكُونُ بَيْنَهُ وَبَيْنَهَا إِلَّا ذِرَاعٌ فَيَسْبِقُ عَلَيْهِ الْكِتَابُ فَيَعْمَلُ بِعَمَلِ أَهْلِ الْجَنَّةِ فَيَدْخُلُهَا.»

رَوَاهُ الْبُخَارِيُّ [رقم ٣٢٠٨]، وَمُسْلِمٌ [رقم ٢٦٤٣].

Abū ʿAbdir-Raḥmān ʿAbdullāh bin Masʿūd رَضِيَ اللَّهُ عَنْهُ reported: The Messenger of Allāh صَلَّى اللَّهُ عَلَيْهِ وَسَلَّمَ, the most truthful, the most trusted, told us, «Verily the creation of each one of you takes place when he is assembled in his mother's womb; for forty days he is a *nuṭfah* (drop of fluid), then he becomes an *ʿalaqah* (clot) for a similar period. Thereafter, he is a *muḍghah* (chewed-out piece of flesh) for a similar period. Then an angel is sent to him, who breathes the *rūḥ* (spirit) into him. This angel is commanded to write four decrees: his provision, his life span, his deeds, and whether he will be among the wretched or the blessed. I swear by Allāh—there is no God but He—one of you performs the deeds of the people of Paradise until there is but an arm's length between him and it, when that which has been written will overtake him so that he performs the deeds of the people of the Hell Fire; And one of you performs the deeds of the people of the Hell Fire until there is but an arm's length between him and it, when that which has been written will overtake him so that he performs the deeds of the people of Paradise and enters therein.»

Al-Bukhārī and *Muslim*.

Summarised Lessons

- This *ḥadīth* is an important and meaningful *ḥadīth* that describes the creation of human beings. As shall be pointed out in the commentary, there are many lessons to be learned from the birth of human beings. Secondly, this *ḥadīth* also points to the belief in Qadar and that Allāh has foreknowledge of what everyone will do in this world.

- The majority of the scholars have understood this *ḥadīth* to mean that the fetus passes through three stages of *nuṭfah*, *ʿalaqah*, and *muḍghah*. Each stage takes forty days, for a total of one hundred and twenty days. This author was forced to adopt an opinion that is different from the majority opinion on this question, although it is not unprecedented. It is never an easy proposition to go against what the great scholars of Islam have stated. The author asks Allāh to forgive him if he is mistaken and to guide him to what is correct.

- The alternate explanation of this *ḥadīth*, which is supported by other narrations from the Prophet صَلَّى ٱللَّٰهُ عَلَيْهِ وَسَلَّمَ and what seems to be medical fact, is that the entire three stages occur during the first forty some-odd days after conception.
- There is nothing explicit about when the *rūḥ* is breathed into the fetus. It definitely takes place at least forty days after conception. Some say that it takes place after 130 days. This author has not ventured to make any conclusion on this point. While a human is still a fetus, an angel records its provisions, life span, deeds, and whether he will be happy or miserable. This is all part of the foreknowledge that Allāh possesses about this creation. The deeds a person is performing at the time of his death are the deeds that will determine whether he is from the people of Paradise or the people of Hell. One cannot rest on his past deeds and think he is going to Paradise. Instead, one must continue to struggle and toil for his most important behaviour is his behaviour at the time of his death. A person may be performing the deeds of the people of Hell and, then, by Allāh's mercy, he is guided to perform the deeds of the people of Paradise. Therefore, he will be from the people of Paradise.

Unfortunately, the opposite can also be true. Such has already been recorded for each human while he was in the womb of his mother. Consensus states that it takes place after 120 days.

الحديث الخامس

Fifth Ḥadīth

'Ibādah and *Bid'ah*

عَنْ أُمِّ الْمُؤْمِنِينَ أُمِّ عَبْدِ اللهِ عَائِشَةَ رَضِيَ اللهُ عَنْهَا قَالَتْ: قَالَ رَسُولُ اللهِ ﷺ «مَنْ أَحْدَثَ فِي أَمْرِنَا هَذَا مَا لَيْسَ مِنْهُ فَهُوَ رَدٌّ.»

رَوَاهُ الْبُخَارِيُّ [رقم ٢٦٩٧]، وَمُسْلِمٌ [رقم ١٧١٨]. وَفِي رِوَايَةٍ لِمُسْلِمٍ «مَنْ عَمِلَ عَمَلًا لَيْسَ عَلَيْهِ أَمْرُنَا فَهُوَ رَدٌّ.»

It is narrated on the authority of the Mother of the Believers, Umm ʿAbdīllah ʿĀʾishah رَضِيَ اللهُ عَنْهُ, that the Messenger of Allāh صَلَّى اللهُ عَلَيْهِ وَسَلَّمَ said, «Whosoever introduces into this affair of ours (Islam) something that does not belong to it is to be rejected.»

Al-Bukhārī and *Muslim*.

The version in *Muslim* reads, "Whosoever performs an action which has no command for it in this religion of ours is to be rejected."

Summarised Lessons

- An act is clearly part of the religion of Islam if it has acceptable evidence for it in the Quran, Sunnah, consensus and what can be derived from those sources.
- If an act is inconsistent with the Quran and Sunnah, it is void and worthless. The act will be rejected by Allāh. It will bear no reward and have no legal effect.
- The one who introduces such an innovation and the one who practices it later are all equal in having their innovation rejected.

الحديث السادس

Sixth Ḥadīth

Doubtful Matters

عَنْ أَبِي عَبْدِ اللّٰهِ النُّعْمَانِ بْنِ بَشِيرٍ رَضِيَ اللهُ عَنْهُمَا، قَالَ: سَمِعْتُ رَسُولَ اللّٰهِ ﷺ يَقُولُ «إِنَّ الْحَلَالَ بَيِّنٌ، وَإِنَّ الْحَرَامَ بَيِّنٌ، وَبَيْنَهُمَا أُمُورٌ مُشْتَبِهَاتٌ لَا يَعْلَمُهُنَّ كَثِيرٌ مِنْ النَّاسِ، فَمَنْ اتَّقَى الشُّبُهَاتِ فَقْد اسْتَبْرَأَ لِدِينِهِ وَعِرْضِهِ، وَمَنْ وَقَعَ فِي الشُّبُهَاتِ وَقَعَ فِي الْحَرَامِ، كَالرَّاعِي يَرْعَى حَوْلَ الْحِمَى يُوشِكُ أَنْ يَرْتَعَ فِيهِ، أَلَا وَإِنَّ لِكُلِّ مَلِكٍ حِمًى، أَلَّا وَإِنَّ حِمَى اللّٰهِ مَحَارِمُهُ، أَلَّا وَإِنَّ فِي الْجَسَدِ مُضْغَةً إِذَا صَلَحَتْ صَلَحَ الْجَسَدُ كُلُّهُ، وَإِذَا فَسَدَتْ فَسَدَ الْجَسَدُ كُلُّهُ، أَلَا وَهِيَ الْقَلْبُ.»

رَوَاهُ الْبُخَارِيُّ [رقم ٥٢] وَمُسْلِمٌ [رقم ١٥٩٩].

On the authority of Abī ʿAbdillah al-Nuʿmān bin Bashīr رَضِيَ اللهُ عَنْهُمَا who said, "I heard the Messenger of Allāh ﷺ say, «Truly, what is lawful is clear, and what is unlawful is clear, and in between the two are matters which are doubtful which many people do not know. He who guards against doubtful things keeps his religion and honour blameless, and he who indulges in doubtful things actually indulges in unlawful things, just as a shepherd who grazes his flock around a pasture will soon graze them in it. Beware, every king has a pasture, and the things Allāh has declared unlawful are His pasture. Beware; in the body there is a flesh; if it is sound, the whole body is sound, and if it is corrupt, the whole body is corrupt, and behold, it is the heart.»"

Al-Bukhārī and *Muslim*.

Summarised Lessons

- The Prophet صَلَّى ٱللَّهُ عَلَيْهِ وَسَلَّمَ clarified all matters of the religion. However, some matters are much clearer than others or clearer to some than to others. Hence, with respect to any individual, all acts can be divided into three categories: things that are clearly permissible, things that are clearly forbidden, and things that lie in between them concerning which a person cannot determine or know if they are permissible or forbidden.

- There will be some scholars who will know

the correct ruling concerning the doubtful matters. However, their number may be quite small.

- A Muslim must decide what to do about doubtful matters. If he decides to take part in them, they may lead him to some acts that are clearly not allowed.
- The pious person will avoid doubtful matters. Hence, his religion or his honour stay above and beyond any kind of suspicion.
- Forbidden acts are Allāh's private pasture. Everyone should do his best to make sure that his *flock* remains away from that private pasture. The only way to ensure that is to remain far away from the private pasture.
- Each Muslim must make sure that his heart is pure and wholesome. The heart is the key to all of one's actions and behaviour. If the heart is pure and wholesome, the person's deeds will be pure and wholesome. If the heart is ill, then that will be reflected in the deeds.
- Staying away from the forbidden and doubtful matters is one of the best ways to protect the heart from becoming diseased or ill.

الحديث السابع

Seventh Ḥadīth

Naṣīḥah (Advice)

عَنْ أَبِي رُقَيَّةَ تَمِيمِ بْنِ أَوْسٍ الدَّارِيِّ رَضِيَ اللَّهُ عَنْهُ أَنَّ النَّبِيَّ صَلَّى اللَّهُ عَلَيْهِ وَسَلَّمَ قَالَ «الدِّينُ النَّصِيحَةُ.» قُلْنَا: لِمَنْ؟ قَالَ «للهِ، وَلِكِتَابِهِ، وَلِرَسُولِهِ، وَلِأَئِمَّةِ الْمُسْلِمِينَ وَعَامَّتِهِمْ.»

رَوَاهُ مُسْلِمٌ [رقم ٥٥].

On the authority of Tamīm al-Dārī رَضِيَ اللَّهُ عَنْهُ that the Prophet صَلَّى اللَّهُ عَلَيْهِ وَسَلَّمَ said, «Religion is *naṣīḥah*.» We said, "To whom?" The Prophet صَلَّى اللَّهُ عَلَيْهِ وَسَلَّمَ said, «To Allāh, His Book, His Messenger, and to the leaders of the Muslims and their common folk.»

Muslim.

Summarised Lessons

- The reality of this religion, the essence of this religion, or a necessary component of this religion is *naṣīḥah*.

- *Naṣīḥah* means that the person has a true feeling of well-wishing for others. He wants what is best for them. He strives for that goal in his actions. The result of that true *naṣīḥah* is the complete brotherhood feeling of Islam.

- *Naṣīḥah* is to be towards Allāh, His Book, His Messengers, the leaders of the Muslims and Muslim people in general.

- Zamarlī has an excellent passage at the end of his booklet on *naṣīḥah* that is fitting as a summary here: I say to the one who is giving *naṣīḥah* (advice), "It is a must upon you that you abide by the conditions and manners of giving advice so that the one who is being given advice will accept it, tend to it, and respect it. It is obligatory that your concern and intention, first and last, be bringing about some good or betterment for your brother; and the driving force behind your act [of advising] must be love and brotherhood. You should never stray from that purpose such that your purpose becomes fame, or being greater than another person, or boasting or acting for show. It is also a must for the one being advised to accept the advice no matter its source, since it is a cause of reform and good for him. He should be kind to the advisor and have respect and love for him. He should not be tough with him or harsh or reject his advice to his face. We must all bear with each other concerning our mistakes and excuse one another as long as our goal and purpose is goodness and reform."

الحديث الثامن

Eighth Ḥadīth

The Concept of *Jihād*

عَنْ ابْنِ عُمَرَ رَضِيَ اللَّهُ عَنْهُمَا أَنَّ رَسُولَ اللَّهِ ﷺ قَالَ «أُمِرْتُ أَنْ أُقَاتِلَ النَّاسَ حَتَّى يَشْهَدُوا أَنْ لَا إِلَهَ إِلَّا اللَّهُ وَأَنَّ مُحَمَّدًا رَسُولُ اللَّهِ، وَيُقِيمُوا الصَّلَاةَ، وَيُؤْتُوا الزَّكَاةَ؛ فَإِذَا فَعَلُوا ذَلِكَ عَصَمُوا مِنِّي دِمَاءَهُمْ وَأَمْوَالَهُمْ إِلَّا بِحَقِّ الْإِسْلَامِ، وَحِسَابُهُمْ عَلَى اللَّهِ تَعَالَى.»

رَوَاهُ الْبُخَارِيُّ [رقم ٢٥] وَمُسْلِمٌ [رقم ٢٢].

ʿAbdullāh bin ʿUmar رَضِيَ اللَّهُ عَنْهُمَا narrated that the Messenger of Allāh صَلَّى اللَّهُ عَلَيْهِ وَسَلَّمَ said, «I have been ordered to fight against the people until they testify that there is no God but Allāh and that Muḥammad is the Messenger of Allāh and until they perform the prayers and pay the Zakāh, and if they do so they will have gained protection from me for their lives and property, unless [they do acts that are punishable] in accordance with Islam, and their reckoning will be with Allāh.»

Al-Bukhārī and *Muslim*.

Summarised Lessons

- This religion of Islam is one that must be spread to the people. Indeed, people must even be fought in order to spread this religion. This is how important it is to spread this religion.
- Once the people embrace Islam, they are no longer to be fought; their wealth and lives become protected.
- A person could possibly perform such a heinous crime that calls for his life to be taken.
- Allāh is the One who knows the Unseen and what is in the hearts. In this world, people are to be treated according to their outward appearance. However, Allāh knows who are the true Muslims and who are the insincere and the hypocrites. Hence, Allāh will judge them accordingly on the Day of Judgement.

الحديث التاسع

Ninth Ḥadīth

Fulfilling the Obligations

عَنْ أَبِي هُرَيْرَةَ عَبْدِ الرَّحْمَنِ بْنِ صَخْرٍ رَضِيَ اللهُ عَنْهُ قَالَ: سَمِعْتُ رَسُولَ اللهِ ﷺ يَقُولُ «مَا نَهَيْتُكُمْ عَنْهُ فَاجْتَنِبُوهُ، وَمَا أَمَرْتُكُمْ بِهِ فَأْتُوا مِنْهُ مَا اسْتَطَعْتُمْ، فَإِنَّمَا أَهْلَكَ الَّذِينَ مِنْ قَبْلِكُمْ كَثْرَةُ مَسَائِلِهِمْ وَاخْتِلَافُهُمْ عَلَى أَنْبِيَائِهِمْ.»

رَوَاهُ الْبُخَارِيُّ [رقم ٧٢٨٨] وَمُسْلِمٌ [رقم ١٣٣٧].

Abū Hurayrah ʿAbdur-Raḥmān bin Ṣakhr reported: I heard the Messenger of Allāh ﷺ say, «Avoid that which I forbid you to do and do that which I command you to do to the best of your capacity. Verily the people before you were destroyed only because of their excessive questioning and their disagreement with their Prophets.»

Al-Bukhārī and *Muslim*.

Summarised Lessons

- If something is prohibited, one must stay away from it completely. The only exception to that is the true case of necessity. Due to necessity, an act may no longer be considered prohibited.
- If something is ordered, one must perform it to the best of his ability. It is not possible to completely and excellently perform everything that one is ordered to do. Hence, the Prophet صَلَّىٰ ٱللَّٰهُ عَلَيْهِ وَسَلَّمَ has stated the cases of prohibition and order in different tones.
- Asking too many questions, beyond what is needed and not with the real intent of application, is blameworthy. It was one of the reasons that prior peoples were destroyed.
- Similarly, differing with any prophet is completely blameworthy. Instead of accepting and submitting, prior peoples showed some form of opposition to what their prophets requested of them. This was the second major cause for their destruction.

الحديث العاشر

Tenth Ḥadīth

Purity

عَنْ أَبِي هُرَيْرَةَ رَضِيَ اللهُ عَنْهُ قَالَ: قَالَ رَسُولُ اللهِ ﷺ «إِنَّ اللهَ طَيِّبٌ لَا يَقْبَلُ إِلَّا طَيِّبًا، وَإِنَّ اللهَ أَمَرَ الْمُؤْمِنِينَ بِمَا أَمَرَ بِهِ الْمُرْسَلِينَ فَقَالَ تَعَالَى ﴿يَٰٓأَيُّهَا ٱلرُّسُلُ كُلُواْ مِنَ ٱلطَّيِّبَٰتِ وَٱعْمَلُواْ صَٰلِحًا﴾ وَقَالَ تَعَالَى ﴿يَٰٓأَيُّهَا ٱلَّذِينَ ءَامَنُواْ كُلُواْ مِن طَيِّبَٰتِ مَا رَزَقْنَٰكُمْ﴾ ثُمَّ ذَكَرَ الرَّجُلَ يُطِيلُ السَّفَرَ أَشْعَثَ أَغْبَرَ يَمُدُّ يَدَيْهِ إِلَى السَّمَاءِ: يَا رَبِّ! يَا رَبِّ! وَمَطْعَمُهُ حَرَامٌ، وَمَشْرَبُهُ حَرَامٌ، وَمَلْبَسُهُ حَرَامٌ، وَغُذِّيَ بِالْحَرَامِ، فَأَنَّى يُسْتَجَابُ لَهُ؟»

رَوَاهُ مُسْلِمٌ [رقم ١٠١٥].

Abū Hurayrah رَضِيَ اللهُ عَنْهُ reported that the Messenger of Allāh صَلَّى اللهُ عَلَيْهِ وَسَلَّمَ said, «Verily Allāh the Exalted is pure. He does not accept but that which is pure. Allāh commands the believers with what He commanded the Messengers. Allāh has said, ﴾O you Messengers! Eat of the good things and act righteously.﴿ (*al-Mu'minūn*: 51–53) And Allāh also said, ﴾O you who believe! Eat of the good things that We have provided you with.﴿ (*al-Baqarah*: 167–172). Then he (the Prophet صَلَّى اللهُ عَلَيْهِ وَسَلَّمَ) mentioned the man who, having journeyed far, is disheveled and dusty and who stretches out his hands to the sky (saying), "O Lord! O Lord!" whilst his food was unlawful, his drink was unlawful, his clothing was unlawful, and he is nourished with unlawful things; so how can he be answered?»

Muslim.

Summarised Lessons

- Abū 'Abdullāh al-Najī made a statement that very closely summarizes the meaning of this *ḥadīth*. He said five characteristics make a deed complete; [These five are] faith by knowing Allāh, knowing the truth, doing deeds purely for Allāh's sake, performing deeds according to the Sunnah and eating only what is permissible. If any one of these characteristics is lacking, the deed will not be raised [to Allāh]. For example, if you know Allāh but do not know the truth, it will not be of benefit in the least. If you know the truth but do not know Allāh, that also will not benefit you. If you know Allāh and know the truth but your deed is not sincere and pure, it will not be of benefit. If you know Allāh, know the truth, perform the act sincerely but it was not according to the Sunnah, it will not be of benefit. If you met all four characteristics but you did not eat from permissible sources, it will also be of no benefit.

- Doing forbidden acts greatly affects one's relationship with Allāh. Although Allāh is ready to respond to the believers' supplications, Allāh may not respond to the one who greatly indulges in forbidden acts—even if he has met all of the manners that are appropriate and beneficial for supplications.

الحديث الحادي عشر

Eleventh Ḥadīth

Leaving Doubt

عَنْ أَبِي مُحَمَّدٍ الْحَسَنِ بْنِ عَلِيِّ بْنِ أَبِي طَالِبٍ سِبْطِ رَسُولِ اللَّهِ ﷺ وَرَيْحَانَتِهِ رَضِيَ اللَّهُ عَنْهُمَا، قَالَ: حَفِظْتُ مِنْ رَسُولِ اللَّهِ ﷺ «دَعْ مَا يُرِيبُكَ إِلَى مَا لَا يُرِيبُكَ.»

رَوَاهُ التِّرْمِذِيُّ [رقم ٢٥٢٠] وَالنَّسَائِيُّ [رقم ٥٧١١] وَقَالَ التِّرْمِذِيُّ: حَدِيثٌ حَسَنٌ صَحِيحٌ.

On the authority of Abū Muḥammad al-Ḥasan bin ʿAlī bin Abī Ṭālib رَضِيَ اللَّهُ عَنْهُمَا, the grandson of the Messenger of Allāh ﷺ, and whom was dearest to him, said, "I committed to memory from the Messenger of Allāh ﷺ (the following words), «Leave that about which you are in doubt for that about which you are in no doubt.»

Al-Tirmidhī and *al-Nasāʾī*. *Al-Tirmidhī* said, "It is a sound and authentic *ḥadīth*."

Summarised Lessons

- A Muslim should be certain of every act he performs. If he has any doubt concerning something, he should leave it for an act concerning which he has no doubt.
- If there is a conflict between something that is known for certain and something that is a matter of conjecture, then that which is known for certain takes precedence over the conjecture. This is an important legal maxim that is applied throughout Islamic *fiqh*.
- One should base all of his life on the things that he is certain and sure about. He should avoid doubtful matters and matters that he is sure are wrong or harmful. This approach to life will lead him to true happiness in both this life and the Hereafter, Allāh willing.
- There is no piety in avoiding something that is clearly and unquestionably permissible. Piety lies in avoiding anything for which there is a true doubt. If someone is avoiding something that is clearly permissible, supposedly as an act of piety, then he is simply following the whisperings of Satan and not the guidance of the Prophet Muḥammad صَلَّى ٱللَّهُ عَلَيْهِ وَسَلَّمَ.

الحديث الثّاني عشر

Twelfth Ḥadīth

Concern with Beneficial Matters

عَنْ أَبِي هُرَيْرَةَ رَضِيَ اللَّهُ عَنْهُ قَالَ: قَالَ رَسُولُ اللهِ ﷺ «مِنْ حُسْنِ إِسْلَامِ الْمَرْءِ تَرْكُهُ مَا لَا يَعْنِيهِ.»

رَوَاهُ التِّرْمِذِيُّ [رقم ٢٣١٨]، وَابْنُ مَاجه [رقم ٣٩٧٦]، وغيرهما. حَدِيثٌ حَسَنٌ.

On the authority of Abū Hurayrah رَضِيَ اللَّهُ عَنْهُ who said that the Messenger of Allāh صَلَّى اللَّهُ عَلَيْهِ وَسَلَّمَ said, «Part of the perfection of someone's Islam is his leaving alone that which does not concern him.»

Al-Tirmidhī (2318), *Ibn Mājah* (3976), and others. It is a *ḥasan ḥadīth*.

Summarised Lessons

- It should be noted that it was concluded that this *ḥadīth* is most likely a weak *ḥadīth*. However, it is definitely close to being *ḥasan*, and that is why it was commented upon in some detail. Allāh knows best.

- If a person avoids what does not concern him, it means that he is only doing things that are of concern and benefit. Hence, by this means, he is on the road to completing and perfecting his Islam.
- All matters can be divided into one of two categories: Either something that is of concern or benefit to the individual or something that is of no concern or no benefit to the individual. An individual can do either one of them. If he does what is of concern to him, he has done well. If he leaves what does not concern him, he has also done well. However, if he leaves what is of concern or he does what is not of concern, then he is following the wrong path.

الحديث الثالث عشر

Thirteenth Ḥadīth

Loving Your Muslim Brother

عَنْ أَبِي حَمْزَةَ أَنَسِ بْنِ مَالِكٍ رَضِيَ اللَّهُ عَنْهُ خَادِمِ رَسُولِ اللَّهِ صَلَّى اللَّهُ عَلَيْهِ وَسَلَّمَ عَنْ النَّبِيِّ صَلَّى اللَّهُ عَلَيْهِ وَسَلَّمَ قَالَ «لَا يُؤْمِنُ أَحَدُكُمْ حَتَّى يُحِبَّ لِأَخِيهِ مَا يُحِبُّ لِنَفْسِهِ.»

رَوَاهُ الْبُخَارِيُّ [رقم ١٣] وَمُسْلِمٌ [رقم ٤٥].

Abū Ḥamzah Anas bin Mālik, who was the servant of the Messenger of Allāh صَلَّى اللَّهُ عَلَيْهِ وَسَلَّمَ, reported that the Prophet صَلَّى اللَّهُ عَلَيْهِ وَسَلَّمَ said, «None of you truly believes until he loves for his brother that which He loves for himself.»

Al-Bukhārī and *Muslim*.

Summarised Lessons

- The true believer loves for his Muslim brother what he loves for himself of good things. Without possessing this quality, one has not yet reached the level of true and complete *Īmān*.

- The true Islamic society—the society of true believers—is one where the relations between its members are built upon love and compassion. This was truly the case among the Companions. Every member works for the good of all of the members of society. Peace and tranquillity are spread throughout such a society. This only comes about when people truly love for each other what they love for themselves.

- The implementation of this *ḥadīth* is not with words only. That is, a person does not simply claim to love his brother and to love for his brother what he loves for himself. It cannot be a case of mere lip service. Instead, as is the case with all true love, that love must be translated into action. In this case, it means action on behalf of one's brother when one has the means to help him or improve his situation.

الحديث الرابع عشر

Fourteenth Ḥadīth

Sacredness of Life, Chastity, and Fidelity

عَنْ ابْنِ مَسْعُودٍ رَضِيَ اللَّهُ عَنْهُ قَالَ: قَالَ رَسُولُ اللهِ ﷺ «لَا يَحِلُّ دَمُ امْرِئٍ مُسْلِمٍ [يشهد أن لا إله إلا الله، وأني رسول الله] إلَّا بِإِحْدَى ثَلَاثٍ: الثَّيِّبُ الزَّانِي، وَالنَّفْسُ بِالنَّفْسِ، وَالتَّارِكُ لِدِينِهِ الْمُفَارِقُ لِلْجَمَاعَةِ.»

رَوَاهُ الْبُخَارِيُّ [رقم ٦٨٧٨] وَمُسْلِمٌ [رقم ١٦٧٦].

On the authority of Ibn Mas'ūd رَضِيَ اللَّهُ عَنْهُ who said that the Messenger of Allāh صَلَّى اللَّهُ عَلَيْهِ وَسَلَّمَ said, «The blood of a Muslim is unlawful, unless he belongs to one of three (classes): a married person who does adultery, a life for a life, and one who is a deserter of his religion, abandoning the community.»

Al-Bukhārī and *Muslim*.

Summarised Lessons

- The life of a Muslim is inviolable and protected by Islamic Law. No one has the right to take their life unless they commit a crime that calls for the death penalty.
- The committing of adultery, murder, and apostasy are such heinous crimes that Islamic Law, which otherwise safeguards life, has deemed that those who commit such crimes no longer deserve to live.
- One of the purposes of the death penalty is to protect the sanctity and lives of all Muslims. As Allāh states about the Law of Retribution, quoted above, ﴾And there is [saving of] life for you in the Law of Equality in punishment, O men of understanding, that you may become pious.﴿ (al-Baqarah: 178–179)

الحديث الخامس عشر

Fifteenth Ḥadīth

Essential Manners through Speech and Courtesy

عَنْ أَبِي هُرَيْرَةَ رَضِيَ اللَّهُ عَنْهُ أَنَّ رَسُولَ اللهِ ﷺ قَالَ:
«مَنْ كَانَ يُؤْمِنُ بِاللهِ وَالْيَوْمِ الْآخِرِ فَلْيَقُلْ خَيْرًا أَوْ
لِيَصْمُتْ، وَمَنْ كَانَ يُؤْمِنُ بِاللهِ وَالْيَوْمِ الْآخِرِ فَلْيُكْرِمْ
جَارَهُ، وَمَنْ كَانَ يُؤْمِنُ بِاللهِ وَالْيَوْمِ الْآخِرِ فَلْيُكْرِمْ
ضَيْفَهُ.»

رَوَاهُ الْبُخَارِيُّ [رقم ٦٠١٨] وَمُسْلِمٌ [رقم ٤٧].

Abū Hurayrah رَضِيَ اللَّهُ عَنْهُ narrated that the Messenger of Allāh صَلَّى اللَّهُ عَلَيْهِ وَسَلَّمَ said, «Let one who believes in Allāh and the Last Day speak good or be silent. And let one who believes in Allāh and the Last Day honour his neighbour. And let one who believes in Allāh and in the Last Day honour his guest.»

Al-Bukhārī and *Muslim*.

Summarised Lessons

- Those people who are true and complete believers can be described by specific characteristics. If one does not have those specific characteristics, it means that in those matters he is not completing his faith and there is room for improvement.
- A true believer will only speak when it is good and beneficial to speak. Otherwise, he would remain silent.
- If a Muslim is not treating his neighbours well, even non-Muslim neighbors, then they are not fulfilling that condition of faith. That is, he has a shortcoming in his *Īmān*.
- If a Muslim is not being generous and courteous to his visitors from out of town, he is not fulfilling one of the obligatory parts of his faith.
- Ibn ʿAbd al-Barr رَحِمَهُ ٱللَّهُ once said, "If a person has three qualities, then there can be no doubt about his intelligence and virtue. [These three qualities are] that he is praised by his neighbors, relatives, and companions."

الحديث السادس عشر

Sixteenth Ḥadīth

Prohibition of Anger

عَنْ أَبِي هُرَيْرَةَ رَضِيَ اللَّهُ عَنْهُ أَنَّ رَجُلًا قَالَ لِلنَّبِيِّ ﷺ أَوْصِنِي. قَالَ «لَا تَغْضَبْ» فَرَدَّدَ مِرَارًا، قَالَ «لَا تَغْضَبْ.»

رَوَاهُ الْبُخَارِيُّ [رقم ٦١١٦].

Abū Hurayrah رَضِيَ اللَّهُ عَنْهُ reported that a man said to the Prophet صَلَّى اللَّهُ عَلَيْهِ وَسَلَّمَ, "Advise me!" The Prophet صَلَّى اللَّهُ عَلَيْهِ وَسَلَّمَ said, «Do not become angry.» The man asked again, and the Prophet صَلَّى اللَّهُ عَلَيْهِ وَسَلَّمَ said, «Do not become angry.»

Al-Bukhārī.

Summarised Lessons

- A Muslim must realize the petty nature of most of the things that he gets angry about. He must weigh getting angry with pleasing Allāh. This will keep him from getting angry, Allāh willing.

- A Muslim must stays away from those things that usually lead him to get angry.
- A Muslim must not act upon his anger when he gets angry. Instead, he should follow those means that will extinguish his anger.
- Al-Ḥasan al-Baṣrī رَحِمَهُ ٱللَّهُ once stated, "There are four characteristics that if one possesses them, Allāh protects him from Satan and forbids him from the fire. [These four are found in] the one who controls himself while in a state of craving, fear, desiring [or lusting], and being angry."

الحديث السابع عشر

Seventeenth Ḥadīth

The Concept of *Iḥsān*

عَنْ أَبِي يَعْلَى شَدَّادِ بْنِ أَوْسٍ رَضِيَ اللَّهُ عَنْهُ عَنْ رَسُولِ اللَّهِ صَلَّى اللَّهُ عَلَيْهِ وَسَلَّمَ قَالَ «إِنَّ اللَّهَ كَتَبَ الْإِحْسَانَ عَلَى كُلِّ شَيْءٍ، فَإِذَا قَتَلْتُمْ فَأَحْسِنُوا الْقِتْلَةَ، وَإِذَا ذَبَحْتُمْ فَأَحْسِنُوا الذِّبْحَةَ، وَلْيُحِدَّ أَحَدُكُمْ شَفْرَتَهُ، وَلْيُرِحْ ذَبِيحَتَهُ.»

رَوَاهُ مُسْلِمٌ [رقم ١٩٥٥].

Abū Ya'lā Shaddād bin Aws رضي الله عنه reported that the Messenger of Allāh صلى الله عليه وسلم said, «Verily, Allāh has enjoined *Iḥsān* with regard to everything. So, when you kill, kill in an excellent way; when you slaughter, slaughter in an excellent way; so every one of you should sharpen his knife, and let the slaughtered animal die comfortably.»

Muslim.

Summarised Lessons

- There is a level of *Iḥsān* which is obligatory in every deed, namely that the deed be done according to Islamic Law and with the proper intention. This is necessary for it to lead to rewards from Allāh. But even beyond that, every true believer should demonstrate *Iḥsān* in every deed he performs.
- When a person slaughters an animal, he should realize that it is a creation and a possession of Allāh that he is slaughtering. One cannot act in any way he wishes toward that animal. He may only act in the way that its true Owner allows and requires. Therefore, he should slaughter the animal in the way that is most beloved to its real Owner.
- *Iḥsān* is even to be demonstrated toward the disbelievers, most notably by praying to Allāh to guide them to the Straight Path.
- Allāh has prescribed excellence and goodness towards everything and in every act.
- Even while carrying out an execution; it should be done in the best way possible.

- One must slaughter an animal with gentleness and compassion.

الحديث الثامن عشر

Eighteenth Ḥadīth

The Concept of *Taqwā*

عَنْ أَبِي ذَرٍّ جُنْدَبِ بْنِ جُنَادَةَ، وَأَبِي عَبْدِ الرَّحْمَنِ مُعَاذِ بْنِ جَبَلٍ رَضِيَ اللهُ عَنْهُمَا عَنْ رَسُولِ اللهِ ﷺ قَالَ: «اتَّقِ اللهَ حَيْثُمَا كُنْتَ، وَأَتْبِعِ السَّيِّئَةَ الْحَسَنَةَ تَمْحُهَا، وَخَالِقِ النَّاسَ بِخُلُقٍ حَسَنٍ.»

رَوَاهُ التِّرْمِذِيُّ [رقم ١٩٨٧] وَقَالَ: حَدِيثٌ حَسَنٌ، وَفِي بَعْضِ النُّسَخِ: حَسَنٌ صَحِيحٌ.

Abū Dharr Jundub bin Junādah and Abū ʿAbd al-Raḥmān Muʿādh bin Jabal رَضِيَ اللهُ عَنْهُمَا reported that the Messenger of Allāh صَلَّى اللهُ عَلَيْهِ وَسَلَّمَ said, «Fear Allāh wherever you may be and follow up an evil deed with a good one which will wipe it out, and behave with excellent character towards people.»

Al-Tirmidhī related it, saying, "It is a *ḥasan ḥadīth*." In some copies he says, "It is *ḥasan* and *ṣaḥīḥ ḥadīth*."

Summarised Lessons

- The concept and importance of *taqwā* also demonstrates the importance of knowledge. The foundation of *taqwā* is to have knowledge of what one must guard against and how to guard against it. To have fear of Allāh requires knowledge of Him—as He is described in the Quran and Sunnah. The more that one has such knowledge, the more he may fear Allāh and have true *taqwā*. Allāh says in the Quran, ﴿It is only those who have knowledge among His slaves that truly fear Allāh﴾ (Fātir: 28).

- One must have *taqwā* of Allāh under all circumstances. For example, wherever he may be, whether he be alone or with others, he must have *taqwā*.

- Even a person of *taqwā* may slip and commit sins. However, he should not persist in those sins. Instead, he should follow them up with good deeds that will wipe them away by the grace and mercy of Allāh.

- An essential characteristic of *taqwā* is to behave with people in a good manner. One should behave towards them in a manner that he likes for them to behave towards him.

الحديث التاسع عشر

Nineteenth Ḥadīth

Allāh's Protection

عَنْ عَبْدِ اللهِ بْنِ عَبَّاسٍ رَضِيَ اللَّهُ عَنْهُمَا قَالَ: كُنْتُ خَلْفَ رَسُولِ اللهِ صَلَّى اللَّهُ عَلَيْهِ وَسَلَّمَ يَوْمًا، فَقَالَ «يَا غُلَامِ! إِنِّي أُعَلِّمُكَ كَلِمَاتٍ: احْفَظْ اللهَ يَحْفَظْكَ، احْفَظْ اللهَ تَجِدْهُ تُجَاهَكَ، إذَا سَأَلْتَ فَاسْأَلْ اللهَ، وَإِذَا اسْتَعَنْتَ فَاسْتَعِنْ بِاللهِ، وَاعْلَمْ أَنَّ الْأُمَّةَ لَوْ اجْتَمَعَتْ عَلَى أَنْ يَنْفَعُوكَ بِشَيْءٍ لَمْ يَنْفَعُوكَ إلَّا بِشَيْءٍ قَدْ كَتَبَهُ اللهُ لَكَ، وَإِنْ اجْتَمَعُوا عَلَى أَنْ يَضُرُّوكَ بِشَيْءٍ لَمْ يَضُرُّوكَ إلَّا بِشَيْءٍ قَدْ كَتَبَهُ اللهُ عَلَيْكَ؛ رُفِعَتْ الْأَقْلَامُ، وَجَفَّتْ الصُّحُفُ.»

رَوَاهُ التِّرْمِذِيُّ [رقم ٢٥١٦] وَقَالَ: حَدِيثٌ حَسَنٌ صَحِيحٌ.

Abū al-ʿAbbās ʿAbdullāh bin ʿAbbās رَضِيَ اللَّهُ عَنْهُمَا reported: One day I was behind the Prophet صَلَّى اللَّهُ عَلَيْهِ وَسَلَّمَ and he said to me, «O young man, I shall teach you some words [of advice]: Be mindful of Allāh, and Allāh will protect you.

Be mindful of Allāh, and you will find Him in front of you. If you ask, ask of Allāh; and if you seek help, seek help from Allāh. Know that even if the nation were to gather together to benefit you with something, they would not benefit you with anything except that which Allāh has already recorded for you, and that if they gather together to harm you with something, they would not be able to harm you with anything except that which Allāh has already recorded against you. The pens have been lifted and the pages have dried.»

Al-Tirmidhī related this and said, "It is a good genuine *ḥadīth*."

Summarised Lessons

- If a person truly obeys Allāh, Allāh will protect him.
- If a person truly obeys Allāh, he will find Allāh with him in the sense that Allāh will be his close friend and protector. Allāh will not leave him alone or leave him for his enemies to devour him.
- If a person finds himself in need to ask someone for anything, he should turn to Allāh and ask from Allāh.
- If a person is in need of help, he should

turn to Allāh alone as Allāh, in reality, is the only one who can help him.

- Everything is by the decree of Allāh. If Allāh decrees something, it will occur. If Allāh does not decree something, it will never occur. Even if all of mankind tries to change that decree, they will never be able to do so.
- The decree has been made by Allāh and the efforts of man cannot change what has already been recorded; the pens have been lifted and the scrolls have dried.
- If a person becomes *known* or beloved to Allāh during his times of ease and comfort, then Allāh will not leave him alone during his times of hardship and difficulties.
- Humans may face situations that are not pleasing to them. If they are patient during those situations, they will be beneficial for them in both this life and the Hereafter.
- If a person is patient, he will be victorious and successful in the end.
- When difficulties arise, the person must realize that relief is in sight.
- Also, when hardships occur, the person

should realize that situations of ease will follow.

- During such affliction and hardships, one should be patient. If he is going to seek help from anyone, he should seek it from Allāh.

الحديث العشرون

Twentieth Ḥadīth

Modesty is from Faith

عَنْ أَبِي مَسْعُودٍ عُقْبَةَ بْنِ عَمْرٍو الْأَنْصَارِيِّ الْبَدْرِيِّ رضي الله عنه قَالَ: قَالَ رَسُولُ اللهِ ﷺ «إِنَّ مِمَّا أَدْرَكَ النَّاسُ مِنْ كَلَامِ النُّبُوَّةِ الْأُولَى: إِذَا لَمْ تَسْتَحِ فَاصْنَعْ مَا شِئْتَ.»

رَوَاهُ الْبُخَارِيُّ [رقم ٣٤٨٣].

Abū Mas'ūd 'Uqbah bin 'Amr al-Anṣārī al-Badrī رَضِيَ اللَّهُ عَنْهُ reported that the Messenger of Allāh صَلَّى اللَّهُ عَلَيْهِ وَسَلَّمَ said, «Among the things that people have found from the words of the previous prophets was: "If you feel no shame, then do as you wish."»

Al-Bukhārī.

Summarised Lessons

- As stated earlier, al-Nawawī رَحِمَهُ ٱللَّهُ says that all of Islam revolves around this *ḥadīth*. This statement can be understood in the following way: An act is either obligatory, recommended, permissible, disapproved, or forbidden. One should be ashamed not to perform the obligatory and recommended deeds. One should also be ashamed to perform the disapproved or forbidden deeds. As for the permissible deeds, one may be shy to perform them or not. Hence, this concept of *ḥayā'* encompasses all of the acts of the religion. Therefore, all of the religion revolves around this *ḥadīth*.

- The characteristic of *ḥayā'* has been encouraged by all of the previous prophets. Indeed, it may be one of the few of their teachings (or the only one) that had been passed on among the people until the time of the Prophet صَلَّى ٱللَّهُ عَلَيْهِ وَسَلَّمَ.

- Although this *ḥadīth* has a number of possible interpretations, the one preferred by the author is: If an act is not shameful in any way, then it is permissible for a Muslim to do it.

الحديث الحادي والعشرون

Twenty-First Ḥadīth

The Concept of *Istiqāmah*

عَنْ أَبِي عَمْرٍو وَقِيلَ: أَبِي عَمْرَةَ سُفْيَانَ بْنِ عَبْدِ اللهِ الثَّقَفِي رَضِيَ اللهُ عَنْهُ قَالَ: قُلْتُ: يَا رَسُولَ اللهِ! قُلْ لِي فِي الْإِسْلَامِ قَوْلًا لَا أَسْأَلُ عَنْهُ أَحَدًا غَيْرَك؛ قَالَ: «قُلْ: آمَنْتُ بِاَللهِ ثُمَّ اسْتَقِمْ.»

رَوَاهُ مُسْلِمٌ [رقم ٣٨].

On the authority of Abū ʿAmr, though others call him Abū ʿAmrah Sufyān bin ʿAbdullāh al-Thaqafī, who reported: I said, "O Messenger of Allāh, tell me something about Islam which I could not ask anyone about save you." He answered: «Say: 'I believe in Allāh,' and then stand firm and be steadfast.»

Muslim.

Summarised Lessons

- Those who follow innovations and heresies have failed in the obligation of *istiqāmah*. *Istiqāmah* implies being upright along the Straight Path. Those who follow innovations have chosen to swerve from that path. They may, thereby, be robbing themselves of the rewards and benefits of *istiqāmah*.

- Al-Ghazzālī رَحِمَهُ ٱللَّهُ stated that the importance and need for *istiqāmah* is so great that Allāh has ordered His servants to recite Sūrah al-Fātiḥah in every *rakʿah* of their prayers. That Sūrah contains a supplication which is, in essence, a prayer for *istiqāmah* or continual guidance to the straight path.

- All of Islam is encompassed in two aspects: (1) the correct belief in Allāh, and (2) remaining firm and steadfast in that correct belief until death.

الحديث الثّاني والعشرون

Twenty-Second Ḥadīth

The Minimum Obligation

عَنْ أَبِي عَبْدِ اللهِ جَابِرِ بْنِ عَبْدِ اللهِ الْأَنْصَارِيّ رضي الله عنهما: أَنَّ رَجُلاً سَأَلَ رَسُولَ اللهِ ﷺ فَقَالَ: أَرَأَيْتَ إِذَا صَلَّيْتَ الْمَكْتُوبَاتِ، وَصُمْتُ رَمَضَانَ، وَأَحْلَلْتُ الْحَلاَلَ، وَحَرَّمْتُ الْحَرَامَ، وَلَمْ أَزِدْ عَلَى ذَلِكَ شَيْئًا؛ أَأَدْخُلُ الْجَنَّةَ؟ قَالَ «نَعَمْ.»

رَوَاهُ مُسْلِمٌ [رقم ١٥].

Abū ʿAbdullāh Jābir bin ʿAbdullāh al-Anṣārī رَضِيَ ٱللَّهُ عَنْهُ reported that a man questioned the Messenger of Allāh صَلَّى ٱللَّهُ عَلَيْهِ وَسَلَّمَ saying, "Do you see, if I pray the prescribed prayers, fast during Ramaḍān, treat the lawful as permissible and treat the forbidden as prohibited, but do nothing more than that, shall I enter Paradise?" He صَلَّى ٱللَّهُ عَلَيْهِ وَسَلَّمَ answered, «Yes.»

[And the meaning of "treat the forbidden as prohibited" is to stay away from it. And the meaning of "treat the lawful as permissible" is to perform them believing that they are permissible.]

Muslim.

Summarised Lessons

- The key to prosperity and entering Paradise is the performance of the obligatory deeds. The voluntary deeds may make up for some shortcomings in the performance of the obligatory deeds and may also raise a person's rank in Paradise, but the essential deeds are the obligatory deeds.
- The prayers and the fast are two of the essential or most important acts of this religion.
- Doing what is permissible and avoiding what is forbidden is also an essential aspect of the religion.
- If a person truly fulfills the above stated essential aspects of the religion, he will enter Paradise by the grace and mercy of Allāh.

الحديث الثالث والعشرون

Twenty-Third Ḥadīth

Freeing One's Soul

عَنْ أَبِي مَالِكٍ الْحَارِثِ بْنِ عَاصِمٍ الْأَشْعَرِيِّ رَضِيَ اللَّهُ عَنْهُ قَالَ: قَالَ رَسُولُ اللَّهِ ﷺ «الطُّهُورُ شَطْرُ الْإِيمَانِ، وَالْحَمْدُ لِلَّهِ تَمْلَأُ الْمِيزَانَ، وَسُبْحَانَ اللَّهِ وَالْحَمْدُ لِلَّهِ تَمْلَآنِ – أَوْ: تَمْلَأُ – مَا بَيْنَ السَّمَاءِ وَالْأَرْضِ، وَالصَّلَاةُ نُورٌ، وَالصَّدَقَةُ بُرْهَانٌ، وَالصَّبْرُ ضِيَاءٌ، وَالْقُرْآنُ حُجَّةٌ لَك أَوْ عَلَيْك، كُلُّ النَّاسِ يَغْدُو، فَبَائِعٌ نَفْسَهُ فَمُعْتِقُهَا أَوْ مُوبِقُهَا.»

رَوَاهُ مُسْلِمٌ [رقم ٢٢٣].

On the authority of Abū Mālik al-Ḥārith bin ʿĀṣim al-Ashʿarī رَضِيَ اللَّهُ عَنْهُ who said that the Messenger of Allāh صَلَّى اللَّهُ عَلَيْهِ وَسَلَّمَ said, «Purification is half of *Īmān*, and [saying] "Praise is for Allāh," fills the scales, and [saying] "Glory be to Allāh," and "Praise be to Allāh," fills the space between the heavens and the earth, and *Ṣalāh* is a light, and *Ṣadaqah* is a proof, and *Ṣabr* is a shining glory, and the Quran is an argument for you or against you. Every person goes out in the morning and sells their soul, thereby setting it free or destroying it.»

Muslim.

Summarised Lessons

- The phrase, "Purification is half of faith," either means that purification, such as ablution, is so essential to the prayer that it becomes like half of the prayer, with the word *faith* meaning prayer here. Or it means that purifying oneself from associating partners with Allāh or from committing sins fulfills half of faith.

- The simple words, *al-ḥamdulillāh*, when said with belief and adherence are very great in Allāh's sight. Indeed, these words fill the scales.

- The words, *subḥānallāh* and *al-ḥamdulillāh*, together are also so great that they fill what is between the heavens and the earth.

- The phrase, "Prayer is a light," means that the effect of prayer is like a light of guidance. Prayer keeps the person away from performing evil deeds. In addition, prayer will be transformed into a light for the person to guide him to Paradise on the Day of Judgement.

- The phrase, "Charity is a proof," means a proof of one's true belief in Allāh. On the Day of Resurrection, when the slave is asked about his wealth and how he spent it, his charity will come as a clear proof that he used his wealth properly.

- Patience is a brightness that every individual needs. Indeed, this brightness is the source of light and guidance. It is this light that guides the person to performing the obligatory deeds, abstaining from evil deeds and behaving properly in the face of every situation he meets.

- The Quran will either be a proof for the individual or a proof against him. There is no third category. Either the person believes in and obeys the Quran or he does not. If he does, it will be a witness on his behalf. If he does not, it will be a witness against him.

- Every day, whether the individual realizes this or not, he is either taking himself closer to his own rescue or to his own destruction. This is an inescapable fact of life. He can either free himself by selling himself to Allāh or he can destroy himself by selling himself to Satan, his lusts or this world.

الحديث الرّابع والعشرون

Twenty-Fourth Ḥadīth

The Prohibition of Injustice

عَنْ أَبِي ذَرٍّ الْغِفَارِيِّ رَضِيَ اللَّهُ عَنْهُ عَنْ النَّبِيِّ ﷺ فِيمَا يَرْوِيهِ عَنْ رَبِّهِ تَبَارَكَ وَتَعَالَى، أَنَّهُ قَالَ: "يَا عِبَادِي: إنِّي حَرَّمْت الظُّلْمَ عَلَى نَفْسِي، وَجَعَلْته بَيْنَكُمْ مُحَرَّمًا؛ فَلَا تَظَالَمُوا. يَا عِبَادِي! كُلُّكُمْ ضَالٌّ إلَّا مَنْ هَدَيْته، فَاسْتَهْدُونِي أَهْدِكُمْ. يَا عِبَادِي! كُلُّكُمْ جَائِعٌ إلَّا مَنْ أَطْعَمْته، فَاسْتَطْعِمُونِي أُطْعِمْكُمْ. يَا عِبَادِي! كُلُّكُمْ عَارٍ إلَّا مَنْ كَسَوْته، فَاسْتَكْسُونِي أَكْسُكُمْ. يَا عِبَادِي! إنَّكُمْ تُخْطِئُونَ بِاللَّيْلِ وَالنَّهَارِ، وَأَنَا أَغْفِرُ الذُّنُوبَ جَمِيعًا؛ فَاسْتَغْفِرُونِي أَغْفِرْ لَكُمْ. يَا عِبَادِي! إنَّكُمْ لَنْ تَبْلُغُوا ضُرِّي فَتَضُرُّونِي، وَلَنْ تَبْلُغُوا نَفْعِي فَتَنْفَعُونِي. يَا عِبَادِي! لَوْ أَنَّ أَوَّلَكُمْ وَآخِرَكُمْ وَإِنْسَكُمْ وَجِنَّكُمْ كَانُوا عَلَى أَتْقَى قَلْبِ رَجُلٍ وَاحِدٍ مِنْكُمْ، مَا زَادَ ذَلِكَ فِي

مُلْكِي شَيْئًا. يَا عِبَادِي! لَوْ أَنَّ أَوَّلَكُمْ وَآخِرَكُمْ وَإِنْسَكُمْ وَجِنَّكُمْ كَانُوا عَلَى أَفْجَرِ قَلْبِ رَجُلٍ وَاحِدٍ مِنْكُمْ، مَا نَقَصَ ذَلِكَ مِنْ مُلْكِي شَيْئًا. يَا عِبَادِي! لَوْ أَنَّ أَوَّلَكُمْ وَآخِرَكُمْ وَإِنْسَكُمْ وَجِنَّكُمْ قَامُوا فِي صَعِيدٍ وَاحِدٍ، فَسَأَلُونِي، فَأَعْطَيْتُ كُلَّ وَاحِدٍ مَسْأَلَتَه، مَا نَقَصَ ذَلِكَ مِمَّا عِنْدِي إِلَّا كَمَا يَنْقُصُ الْمِخْيَطُ إِذَا أُدْخِلَ الْبَحْرَ. يَا عِبَادِي! إِنَّمَا هِيَ أَعْمَالُكُمْ أُحْصِيهَا لَكُمْ، ثُمَّ أُوَفِّيكُمْ إِيَّاهَا؛ فَمَنْ وَجَدَ خَيْرًا فَلْيَحْمَدْ اللهَ، وَمَنْ وَجَدَ غَيْرَ ذَلِكَ فَلَا يَلُومَن إِلَّا نَفْسَهُ."

رَوَاهُ مُسْلِمٌ [رقم ٢٥٧٧].

It was related on the authority of Abū Dharr al-Ghifārī رَضِيَ اللَّهُ عَنْهُ that the Prophet صَلَّى اللَّهُ عَلَيْهِ وَسَلَّمَ said, of what he related from his Lord, Magnified and Exalted be He, Who said, "O My servants, I have made oppression unlawful for Me and I have made it unlawful amongst yourselves, so do no commit oppression. O My servants, all of you are astray except for those whom I guide, therefore seek guidance from Me, I will guide you. O My servants, all of you are hungry except for those whom I feed, therefore seek food from Me, I will feed you.

O My servants, all of you are naked except for those whom I clothe, therefore seek clothing from Me, I will clothe you.

O My servants, Indeed you sin by night and day and I forgive all sins, therefore seek forgiveness from Me, I will forgive you. O My servants, you will not be able to harm Me so as to bring any harm to Me, and you will not be able to benefit me so as to bring any benefit to Me. O My servants, if the first of you and the last of you and the human of you and the jinn of you were the most pious as the most pious heart of anyone amongst you, it will not add anything to My Kingdom. O My servants, if the first of you and the last of you and the human of you and the jinn of you were the most wicked heart of anyone amongst you, it will not decrease anything from My Kingdom.

O My servants, if the first of you and the last of you and the human of you, and the jinn of you were to gather together on one level land and ask of Me, and if I were to give each one of them what they asked, that will not in any way decrease what I have any more than what a needle decreases what is in the ocean when it is put into it. O My servants, it is only these deeds of yours which I am recording for you then I shall recompense you for them, so he who finds good should praise Allāh and the one who finds other than that should not blame anyone but himself."

Muslim.

Summarised Lessons

- Allāh has decreed for Himself that He will not commit any form of wrongdoing or injustice.
- Allāh has also prohibited all forms of *ẓulm* or wrongdoing for His slaves.
- All of mankind is lost and astray except for those whom Allāh has guided. Hence, one must turn to Allāh and Allāh alone for guidance. Allāh will guide those who sincerely turn to Him for guidance.
- All of mankind is hungry and naked save for those whom Allāh feeds and clothes. Hence, everyone must turn to Allāh for their sustenance and provisions as He is the only One who can grant such.
- Mankind constantly sins against its Lord. They are, therefore, in need of forgiveness. The only One who can offer forgiveness is Allāh. If humans sincerely repent and turn to Allāh for forgiveness, Allāh will forgive them.

- Mankind cannot help nor harm Allāh in any way. Allāh is Self-Sufficient and free of any wants. No matter how pious or evil humans are, they do not increase or decrease Allāh's dominion in any way.

- Allāh's dominion is so great that He could give all of the creation all that it could possibly ask for and yet that would not decrease Allāh's dominion in the least.

- Allāh is recording and preserving all of the deeds of mankind. Allāh does no injustice whatsoever. All deeds will be presented exactly on the Day of Resurrection and everyone will be fully and fairly recompensed for them.

- If the end result of one's deeds is good, the person should praise and thank Allāh for guiding him and helping him perform the good deeds.

- If the end result of one's deeds is evil, the person has no one to blame but himself. Allāh is not wronging him in the least, but his own deeds and his own choice of remaining astray are what led him to his final resting place.

الحديث الخامس والعشرون
Twenty-Fifth Ḥadīth
The Concept of *Ṣadaqah*

عَنْ أَبِي ذَرٍّ رَضِيَ اللَّهُ عَنْهُ أَيْضًا أَنَّ نَاسًا مِنْ أَصْحَابِ رَسُولِ اللَّهِ ﷺ قَالُوا لِلنَّبِيِّ ﷺ: يَا رَسُولَ اللَّهِ ذَهَبَ أَهْلُ الدُّثُورِ بِالْأُجُورِ؛ يُصَلُّونَ كَمَا نُصَلِّي، وَيَصُومُونَ كَمَا نَصُومُ، وَيَتَصَدَّقُونَ بِفُضُولِ أَمْوَالِهِمْ. قَالَ «أَوَلَيْسَ قَدْ جَعَلَ اللَّهُ لَكُمْ مَا تَصَّدَّقُونَ؟ إِنَّ بِكُلِّ تَسْبِيحَةٍ صَدَقَةً، وَكُلِّ تَكْبِيرَةٍ صَدَقَةً، وَكُلِّ تَحْمِيدَةٍ صَدَقَةً، وَكُلِّ تَهْلِيلَةٍ صَدَقَةً، وَأَمْرٌ بِمَعْرُوفٍ صَدَقَةٌ، وَنَهْيٌ عَنْ مُنْكَرٍ صَدَقَةٌ، وَفِي بُضْعِ أَحَدِكُمْ صَدَقَةٌ.» قَالُوا: يَا رَسُولَ اللَّهِ أَيَأْتِي أَحَدُنَا شَهْوَتَهُ وَيَكُونُ لَهُ فِيهَا أَجْرٌ؟ قَالَ «أَرَأَيْتُمْ لَوْ وَضَعَهَا فِي حَرَامٍ أَكَانَ عَلَيْهِ وِزْرٌ؟ فَكَذَلِكَ إِذَا وَضَعَهَا فِي الْحَلَالِ، كَانَ لَهُ أَجْرٌ.»

رَوَاهُ مُسْلِمٌ [رقم ١٠٠٦].

Abū Dharr رَضِيَ ٱللَّهُ عَنْهُ reported that some of the Companions of the Messenger of Allāh صَلَّى ٱللَّهُ عَلَيْهِ وَسَلَّمَ said to him, "O Messenger of Allāh, the rich have taken all the rewards. They observe the prayer as we do, and they keep the fasts as we do, and they give *ṣadaqah* from their surplus wealth." Upon this he صَلَّى ٱللَّهُ عَلَيْهِ وَسَلَّمَ said, «Has Allāh not made for you (a course) by which you can also do *ṣadaqah*? Verily, every *tasbīḥ* is a *ṣadaqah*, every *takbīr* is a *ṣadaqah*, every *taḥmīd* is a *ṣadaqah*, every *tahlīl* is a *ṣadaqah*, enjoining the good is a *ṣadaqah*, forbidding the evil is a *ṣadaqah*, and one of you having sexual intercourse (with your wife) is a *ṣadaqah*.» They رَضِيَ ٱللَّهُ عَنْهُمْ said, "O Messenger of Allāh, is there reward for him who satisfies his passion among us?" He صَلَّى ٱللَّهُ عَلَيْهِ وَسَلَّمَ said, «Tell me, if he were to fulfill it to something forbidden, would it not be a sin upon him? Similarly, if he were to fulfill it lawfully, it would be a reward for him.»

***Muslim*.**

Summarised Lessons

- The path to pleasing Allāh is very wide and affording. If a person is not able or good at performing one type of good deed that is pleasing to Allāh, he may be able to fulfill other important deeds that are just as pleasing to Allāh. The important point is that one should not miss the opportunity to please Allāh by performing the deeds that are within his ability.

- Virtually everyone has the ability to perform some acts of "charity." There is no excuse for any Muslim not to perform the simple acts of charity that may bring him great reward from Allāh.

- A Muslim should never overlook any good deed. Even a deed such as smiling when meeting one's brother is very pleasing to Allāh and will be recorded for the person as an act of charity.

- Everyone has some acts of charity available to him. For example, the words of *dhikr* are acts of charity as is ordering good and eradicating evil.

- Every permissible deed that a person performs with the proper intention will be considered an act of charity for him and he will be rewarded for it.

- Punishment from Allāh is the result of doing what is forbidden.

الحديث السادس والعشرون

Twenty-Sixth Ḥadīth

Ṣadaqah is Enjoined upon Every Joint

عَنْ أَبِي هُرَيْرَةَ رَضِيَ اللهُ عَنْهُ قَالَ: قَالَ رَسُولُ اللهِ ﷺ «كُلُّ سُلَامَى مِنَ النَّاسِ عَلَيْهِ صَدَقَةٌ، كُلَّ يَوْمٍ تَطْلُعُ فِيهِ الشَّمْسُ تَعْدِلُ بَيْنَ اثْنَيْنِ صَدَقَةٌ، وَتُعِينُ الرَّجُلَ فِي دَابَّتِهِ فَتَحْمِلُهُ عَلَيْهَا أَوْ تَرْفَعُ لَهُ عَلَيْهَا مَتَاعَهُ صَدَقَةٌ، وَالْكَلِمَةُ الطَّيِّبَةُ صَدَقَةٌ، وَبِكُلِّ خُطْوَةٍ تَمْشِيهَا إِلَى الصَّلَاةِ صَدَقَةٌ، وَتُمِيطُ الْأَذَى عَنِ الطَّرِيقِ صَدَقَةٌ.»

رَوَاهُ الْبُخَارِيُّ [رقم ٢٩٨٩] وَمُسْلِمٌ [رقم ١٠٠٩].

Abū Hurayrah رَضِيَ اللهُ عَنْهُ reported that the Messenger of Allāh صَلَّى اللهُ عَلَيْهِ وَسَلَّمَ said, «On every person's small bones, there is a *ṣadaqah* every day the sun rises. Doing justice between two people is *ṣadaqah*, assisting a man to mount his animal, lifting him onto it, or carrying his belongings onto it is a *ṣadaqah*, a good word is a *ṣadaqah*, every step you take towards the prayer is a *ṣadaqah*, and removing harmful things from the path is a ṣadaqah.»

Al-Bukhārī and *Muslim*.

Summarised Lessons

- The small bones in a person's hand and foot, in particular, and all of the bones and joints in a body, in general, form part of the marvelous creation that Allāh has created. This marvelous creation and its magnificent workings are, in themselves, great bounties. Everyone should be thankful to Allāh each and every day for such bounties.

- The gratefulness that one shows is not simply by expressing a statement. Instead, it must also be shown in acts of charity toward others. These acts of charity do not require wealth and are available to almost everyone.

- Bringing about justice between two people, helping a man get on his mount, or placing his belongings on his conveyance, a good word, and every step one takes to the mosque are just some of the acts of charity that a Muslim should seek to perform.

- One can understand from this *ḥadīth* that any act of kindness toward others is an act of charity. This exemplifies the personality of a believer. He realizes that he has received great and wonderful blessings from Allāh. In gratitude to Allāh, he uses those blessings to improve himself (such as making *dhikr*) and to help and improve those around him. Indeed, he uses them to improve the whole world. He never discounts any act of kindness because no matter how many such acts he performs in gratitude to Allāh, he realizes that he can never match the great blessings that he has received from Allāh.

الحديث السابع والعشرون

Twenty-Seventh Ḥadīth

Our Internal Control System

عَنْ النَّوَّاسِ بْنِ سَمْعَانَ رَضِيَ اللَّهُ عَنْهُ عَنْ النَّبِيِّ ﷺ قَالَ «الْبِرُّ حُسْنُ الْخُلُقِ، وَالْإِثْمُ مَا حَاكَ فِي صَدْرِك، وَكَرِهْت أَنْ يَطَّلِعَ عَلَيْهِ النَّاسُ.» [١]

وَعَنْ وَابِصَةَ بْنِ مَعْبَدٍ رَضِيَ اللَّهُ عَنْهُ قَالَ: أَتَيْتُ رَسُولَ اللهِ ﷺ فَقَالَ: «جِئْتَ تَسْأَلُ عَنْ الْبِرِّ؟» قُلْتُ: نَعَمْ. فقَالَ «استفت قلبك، الْبِرُّ مَا اطْمَأَنَّتْ إلَيْهِ النَّفْسُ، وَاطْمَأَنَّ إلَيْهِ الْقَلْبُ، وَالْإِثْمُ مَا حَاكَ فِي النَّفْسِ وَتَرَدَّدَ فِي الصَّدْرِ، وَإِنْ أَفْتَاك النَّاسُ وَأَفْتَوْك.» [٢]

[١] رَوَاهُ مُسْلِمٌ [رقم ٢٥٥٣].

[٢] حَدِيثٌ حَسَنٌ، رَوَيْنَاهُ فِي مُسْنَدَي الْإِمَامَيْنِ أَحْمَدَ بْنِ حَنْبَلٍ [رقم ٤/٢٢٧] وَالدَّارِمِيّ [٢/٢٤٦] بِإِسْنَادٍ حَسَنٍ.

Al-Nawwās bin Samʿān رَضِيَ ٱللَّهُ عَنْهُ reported that the Prophet صَلَّى ٱللَّهُ عَلَيْهِ وَسَلَّمَ said, «Righteousness is good character, and sin is that which wavers in your heart and which you do not want people to know about.» [1]

And as narrated by Wābiṣah bin Maʿbad رَضِيَ ٱللَّهُ عَنْهُ who said, "I came to the Messenger of Allāh صَلَّى ٱللَّهُ عَلَيْهِ وَسَلَّمَ and he said, «You have come to ask about righteousness?» I answered 'Yes.' He said, «Consult your heart. Righteousness is that about which the soul feels tranquil and the heart feels tranquil, and sin is what creates restlessness in the soul and moves to and from the breast, even though people give you their verdict and continue to give you their verdict.»" [2]

[1] *Muslim*.

[2] A good *ḥadīth* transmitted from the *Musnads* of the two Imams, *Aḥmad bin Ḥanbal* and *al-Dārimī*.

Summarised Lessons

- Before a believer performs any act that is not clearly righteous or sinful, he should look to his heart and see what he feels about that act. If his heart feels fine with it, he should do it. If his heart is uncomfortable with it, he should leave it.

- "The main or essential aspect of righteousness is good character." or, "Righteousness is good character."
- Sin has a direct effect on a pious person's heart. It makes his soul uneasy and wavering.
- Another sign of sin is that a person dislikes to have people witness the act.
- A believer should consult his heart before performing a deed. If his heart feels uncomfortable about it, he should avoid it, even if the people give him verdicts that there is nothing wrong with the act.

الحديث الثّامن والعشرون

Twenty-Eighth Ḥadīth

Adhering to the *Sunnah* and avoiding *Bid'ah*

عَنْ أَبِي نَجِيحٍ الْعِرْبَاضِ بْنِ سَارِيَةَ رَضِيَ اللَّهُ عَنْهُ قَالَ: وَعَظَنَا رَسُولُ اللَّهِ ﷺ مَوْعِظَةً وَجِلَتْ مِنْهَا الْقُلُوبُ، وَذَرَفَتْ مِنْهَا الْعُيُونُ، فَقُلْنَا: يَا رَسُولَ اللَّهِ! كَأَنَّهَا مَوْعِظَةُ مُوَدِّعٍ فَأَوْصِنَا، قَالَ ﷺ «أُوصِيكُمْ بِتَقْوَى اللَّهِ، وَالسَّمْعِ وَالطَّاعَةِ وَإِنْ تَأَمَّرَ عَلَيْكُمْ عَبْدٌ، فَإِنَّهُ مَنْ يَعِشْ مِنْكُمْ فَسَيَرَى اخْتِلَافًا كَثِيرًا، فَعَلَيْكُمْ بِسُنَّتِي وَسُنَّةِ الْخُلَفَاءِ الرَّاشِدِينَ الْمَهْدِيِّينَ، عَضُّوا عَلَيْهَا بِالنَّوَاجِذِ، وَإِيَّاكُمْ وَمُحْدَثَاتِ الْأُمُورِ؛ فَإِنَّ كُلَّ بِدْعَةٍ ضَلَالَةٌ.»

رَوَاهُ أَبُو دَاوُدَ [رقم ٤٦٠٧] وَالتِّرْمِذِيُّ [رقم ٢٦٦] وَقَالَ: حَدِيثٌ حَسَنٌ صَحِيحٌ.

It was narrated on the authority of Abū Najīḥ al-ʿIrbāḍ bin Sāriyah رَضِيَ اللَّهُ عَنْهُ who said, "The Messenger of Allāh صَلَّى اللَّهُ عَلَيْهِ وَسَلَّمَ delivered an admonition that made our hearts fearful and our eyes tearful. We said, 'O Messenger of Allāh, it is as if this were a farewell sermon, so advise us.' He صَلَّى اللَّهُ عَلَيْهِ وَسَلَّمَ said, «I enjoin you to have *taqwā* of Allāh and that you listen and obey, even if a slave is made a ruler over you. He amongst you who lives long enough will see many differences. So for you is to observe my Sunnah and the Sunnah of the Rightly-guided Caliphs. Hold on to them with your molar teeth. And beware of newly-introduced matters, for every *bidʿah* is an error.»"

Abū Dāwūd and *al-Tirmidhī*, who said it is an authentic *ḥadīth*.

Summarised Lessons

- The Prophet صَلَّى اللَّهُ عَلَيْهِ وَسَلَّمَ used to give speeches, admonitions, and words of advice to his Companions. The effect on the Companions was that their hearts would become fearful and their eyes tearful.
- Knowing the Sunnah of the Prophet صَلَّى اللَّهُ عَلَيْهِ وَسَلَّمَ and what is consistent with it is one of the most important matters that

one must learn. It is the way of salvation. Similarly, knowing and recognizing innovations and heresies, which are on the path to destruction, is also one of the important topics to learn. One of the best ways to avoid heresies is to know them and where and how they appear. The one who does not know what is evil often falls into such evil. Many people are ignorant of this matter and fail to learn the Sunnah or recognize what are innovations and heresies. Hence, they become lost without realizing it at all.

- He ordered them to listen to and obey the ruler, regardless of who the ruler might be.

- He warned them of future times in which there would be lots of differences and confusion. He gave them the key to being rescued from those differences: stick to the Sunnah of the Prophet صَلَّىٱللَّهُعَلَيْهِوَسَلَّمَ and those who adhered to his way. Do not stray from this path in any way. Adhere to it as if biting onto it with one's molar teeth.

- The Prophet صَلَّىٱللَّهُعَلَيْهِوَسَلَّمَ then warned them about the newly invented matters that were going to appear. He stated that all of them are misguidance and lead one astray from the Straight Path, the path of the Prophet صَلَّىٱللَّهُعَلَيْهِوَسَلَّمَ.

الحديث التّاسع والعشرون

Twenty-Ninth Ḥadīth

Deeds that Lead to Paradise

عَنْ مُعَاذِ بْنِ جَبَلٍ رَضِيَ اللهُ عَنْهُ قَالَ: قُلْتُ يَا رَسُولَ اللهِ! أَخْبِرْنِي بِعَمَلٍ يُدْخِلُنِي الْجَنَّةَ وَيُبَاعِدُنِي مِنَ النَّارِ، قَالَ «لَقَدْ سَأَلْتَ عَنْ عَظِيمٍ، وَإِنَّهُ لَيَسِيرٌ عَلَى مَنْ يَسَّرَهُ اللهُ عَلَيْهِ: تَعْبُدُ اللهَ لَا تُشْرِكْ بِهِ شَيْئًا، وَتُقِيمُ الصَّلَاةَ، وَتُؤْتِي الزَّكَاةَ، وَتَصُومُ رَمَضَانَ، وَتَحُجُّ الْبَيْتَ، ثُمَّ قَالَ: أَلَا أَدُلُّكَ عَلَى أَبْوَابِ الْخَيْرِ؟ الصَّوْمُ جُنَّةٌ، وَالصَّدَقَةُ تُطْفِئُ الْخَطِيئَةَ كَمَا يُطْفِئُ الْمَاءُ النَّارَ، وَصَلَاةُ الرَّجُلِ فِي جَوْفِ اللَّيْلِ، ثُمَّ تَلَا ﴿تَتَجَافَىٰ جُنُوبُهُمْ عَنِ ٱلْمَضَاجِعِ﴾ حَتَّى بَلَغَ ﴿يَعْمَلُونَ﴾، ثُمَّ قَالَ: أَلَا أُخْبِرُكَ بِرَأْسِ الْأَمْرِ وَعَمُودِهِ وَذُرْوَةِ سَنَامِهِ؟» قُلْتُ: بَلَى يَا رَسُولَ اللهِ. قَالَ «رَأْسُ الْأَمْرِ الْإِسْلَامُ، وَعَمُودُهُ الصَّلَاةُ، وَذُرْوَةُ سَنَامِهِ الْجِهَادُ، ثُمَّ قَالَ: أَلَا

أُخْبِرُك بِمَلَاكِ ذَلِكَ كُلِّهِ؟» فقُلْتُ: بَلَى يَا رَسُولَ اللّٰهِ! فَأَخَذَ بِلِسَانِهِ وَقَالَ «كُفَّ عَلَيْك هَذَا.» قُلْت: يَا نَبِيَّ اللّٰهِ وَإِنَّا لَمُؤَاخَذُونَ بِمَا نَتَكَلَّمُ بِهِ؟ فَقَالَ «ثَكِلَتْك أُمُّك وَهَلْ يَكُبُّ النَّاسَ عَلَى وُجُوهِهِمْ – أَوْ قَالَ عَلَى مَنَاخِرِهِمْ – إلَّا حَصَائِدُ أَلْسِنَتِهِمْ؟!»

رَوَاهُ التِّرْمِذِيُّ [رقم ٢٦١٦] وَقَالَ: حَدِيثٌ حَسَنٌ صَحِيحٌ.

From Muʿādh bin Jabal رضي الله عنه who said: I said, "O Messenger of Allāh, tell me of a deed which will take me into Paradise and will keep me away from the Hell-fire." He صلى الله عليه وسلم said, «You have asked me about a great matter, yet it is, indeed, an easy matter for him whom Allāh makes it easy for. (It is) that you worship Allāh without associating anything with Him, that you perform the prayers, that you pay the *Zakāh*, that you fast during Ramaḍān, and that you make the pilgrimage to the House.» Then he صلى الله عليه وسلم said, «Shall I not guide you to the gates of goodness? Fasting is a shield, *ṣadaqah* extinguishes sin as water extinguishes fire, and a man's prayer in the middle of the night.» Then he recited: ﴿Who forsake their beds to cry unto their Lord in fear and hope, and spend of what We have bestowed on them. No soul knows what is kept hidden for them of joy, as a reward for what they used to do.﴾ (Sajdah: 16–17)

Then he said, «Shall I not also tell you of the peak of the matter, its pillar, and its topmost part?» I said, "Yes, O Messenger of Allāh." He ﷺ said, «The peak of the matter is Islam (submission to Allāh), the pillar is prayer; and its topmost part is *jihād*.» Then he ﷺ said, «And shall I not tell you of the controlling of all that?» I said, "Yes, O Messenger of Allāh." So he ﷺ took hold of his tongue and said, «Restrain this.» I said, "O Prophet of Allāh, will we be held accountable for what we say?" He ﷺ said, «May your mother be bereft of you! Is there anything that topples people on their faces (or he said, on their noses) into the Hell-fire other than the jests of their tongues?»

Related by *al-Tirmidhī*, who said it was a fine and sound *ḥadīth*.

Summarised Lessons

- The Companions were very anxious to know the key to entering Paradise and escaping the Hell-fire. Hence, they asked the Prophet ﷺ on numerous occasions to guide them to this goal.

- This question is a great matter. However, if Allāh makes it easy for someone, then it will become easy for him.
- The key to entering Paradise is the fulfillment of the five pillars of Islam.
- Beyond entering Paradise, the Prophet ﷺ explained the keys to the great rewards in Paradise. These keys are voluntary fasts, which are a shield, charity, and prayers during the late night, which extinguish sins.
- The main aspect of the issue of entering Paradise and escaping Hell is in the submission to Allāh. The pillar or the foundation to that submission is prayer. Its apex or loftiest aspect is *jihād* in the way of Allāh.
- Controlling one's tongue is what can control one's acts to lead a person to Paradise and save him from the Hell-fire.
- The greatest reason for people being thrown into the Hell-fire is from the effects of their tongues.

الحديث الثلاثون

Thirtieth Ḥadīth

Transgressing the Limits

عَنْ أَبِي ثَعْلَبَةَ الْخُشَنِيِّ جُرْثُومِ بن نَاشِبٍ رَضِيَ اللَّهُ عَنْهُ عَنْ رَسُولِ اللهِ ﷺ قَال «إِنَّ اللَّهَ تَعَالَى فَرَضَ فَرَائِضَ فَلَا تُضَيِّعُوهَا، وَحَدَّ حُدُودًا فَلَا تَعْتَدُوهَا، وَحَرَّمَ أَشْيَاءَ فَلَا تَنْتَهِكُوهَا، وَسَكَتَ عَنْ أَشْيَاءَ رَحْمَةً لَكُمْ غَيْرَ نِسْيَانٍ فَلَا تَبْحَثُوا عَنْهَا.»

حَدِيثٌ حَسَنٌ، رَوَاهُ الدَّارَقُطْنِيّ فِي "سننه" [١٨٤/٤] وَغَيْرُهُ.

It was narrated on the authority of Abū Thaʿlabah al-Khushanī Jurthūm bin Nāshir رَضِيَ اللَّهُ عَنْهُ, that the Messenger of Allāh صَلَّى اللَّهُ عَلَيْهِ وَسَلَّمَ said, «Verily, Allāh Most High has prescribed the obligatory deeds, so do not neglect them, He has set certain limits, so do not transgress them, He has forbidden certain things, so do not indulge in them, and He is silent about certain things, as an act of mercy to you, not out of forgetfulness, so do not go enquiring into these.»

Related by *al-Dāraquṭnī* and others. Al-Nawawī said this is a *ḥasan ḥadīth*.

General Comments

This *ḥadīth* is a weak *ḥadīth*. Therefore, there is no need to discuss it in detail. However, it should be pointed out that the commentators do not take this *ḥadīth* at face value. In other words, they do not say that every deed concerning which Allāh was silent must be permissible or cannot be asked about or researched. There are many acts possible today that are not mentioned in the Quran or Sunnah while it is clear that they could not possibly be permissible or it is equally clear that their ruling needs to be researched. For this reason, the scholars gave a number of different explanations for the last part of this *ḥadīth*, «And He has been silent about some things, out of mercy upon you and not out of forgetfulness, so do not seek after them.» Al-Baytār has summed up the three different possible explanations as follows:

1. The prohibition was something particular for the time of the Prophet ﷺ. As was discussed in the summarised lessons of Ḥadīth 9, there was a general prohibition

of asking the Prophet صَلَّى ٱللَّٰهُ عَلَيْهِ وَسَلَّمَ concerning matters that were not yet discussed in the Quran and Sunnah.

2. A second interpretation is that the prohibition is for all times but it is particular with respect to the kinds of research and questioning prohibited. It is only with respect to the difficult, detailed, impractical, or irrelevant questions. These are the types of matters that one should not ask about. In general, they do not affect a person's actions and may lead to confusion more than anything else.

3. The third interpretation is that the prohibition is with respect to the general masses only and not with respect to the scholars. The laymen may get into heated debates and discussions without any fruitful results. They are not the people who should be debating or discussing issues that are not clearly discussed in the Quran and Sunnah. This role is left to the scholars only. It is the scholars' job to research such questions and then to give their conclusions and rulings to the general people. It should also be noted that this *ḥadīth* is used by the Ẓāhirīs (Literalists) to support their contention that analogy is not valid and that one must follow the apparent meaning of the texts only. Nonetheless, this is a weak *ḥadīth*

and, therefore, cannot be used to support their contention. In addition, there are many other clear evidences that support the use of analogy and so, even if one assumes that this *ḥadīth* is authentic, one would be forced to interpret it in such a way that it does not forbid analogy.

الحديث الحادي والثلاثون

Thirty-First Ḥadīth

The Concept of *Zuhd*

عَنْ أَبِي الْعَبَّاسِ سَهْلِ بْنِ سَعْدٍ السَّاعِدِيِّ رَضِيَ اللَّهُ عَنْهُ قَالَ: جَاءَ رَجُلٌ إِلَى النَّبِيِّ ﷺ فَقَالَ: يَا رَسُولَ اللّٰهِ! دُلَّنِي عَلَى عَمَلٍ إِذَا عَمِلْتُهُ أَحَبَّنِي اللّٰهُ وَأَحَبَّنِي النَّاسُ؛ فَقَالَ «ازْهَدْ فِي الدُّنْيَا يُحِبُّكَ اللّٰهُ، وَازْهَدْ فِيمَا عِنْدَ النَّاسِ يُحِبُّكَ النَّاسُ.»

حَدِيثٌ حَسَنٌ، رَوَاهُ ابْنُ مَاجَهْ [رقم ٤١٠٢] وَغَيْرُهُ بِأَسَانِيدَ حَسَنَةٍ.

On the authority of Abū al-ʿAbbās Sahl bin Saʿad al-Sāʿidī who said, "A man came to the Prophet صَلَّى ٱللَّهُ عَلَيْهِ وَسَلَّمَ and said, 'O Messenger of Allāh, direct me to an act which if I do it, Allāh will love me and people will love me.' He صَلَّى ٱللَّهُ عَلَيْهِ وَسَلَّمَ answered, «Be indifferent to the world and Allāh will love you; be indifferent to what people possess and people will love you.»

A fine *ḥadīth* related by *Ibn Mājah* and others with good chains of authority.

General Comments

This *ḥadīth* is weak. Therefore, it will not be discussed in detail. However, a few points concerning the correct understanding of *Zuhd* (Islamic asceticism) are in order. First, *Zuhd* does not imply abandoning this world and not working for one's needs in this world. The early scholar Abū Idrīs al-Khawlānī said, "*Zuhd* in this world does not mean forbidding what is permissible or wasting wealth. *Zuhd* with respect to this world is only where a person puts more trust in what is with Allāh than what is in his own hand. If he is afflicted with a calamity [by losing something of this world], he is more hopeful for its reward and what is stored for him in the Hereafter than if it were to have remained with him." Two important concepts are mentioned in this statement and both of them are dealing with the actions of the heart. This is because *Zuhd* is an action of the heart and not an outward action. Sulaymān al-Dārānī said, "Do not testify that anyone has *Zuhd*, for *Zuhd* is in the heart [and cannot be witnessed by others]."

الحديث الثاني والثلاثون

Thirty-Second Ḥadīth

Avoiding Harmful Acts

عَنْ أَبِي سَعِيدٍ سَعْدِ بْنِ مَالِكِ بْنِ سِنَانٍ الْخُدْرِيّ رضي الله عنه أَنَّ رَسُولَ اللهِ ﷺ قَالَ «لَا ضَرَرَ وَلَا ضِرَارَ.»

حَدِيثٌ حَسَنٌ، رَوَاهُ ابْنُ مَاجَهْ [رقم ٢٣٤١] وَالدَّارَقُطْنِيّ [رقم ٢٢٨/٤] وَغَيْرُهُمَا مُسْنَدًا. وَرَوَاهُ مَالِكٌ [٧٤٦/٢] فِي "الْمُوَطَّإِ" عَنْ عَمْرِو بْنِ يَحْيَى عَنْ أَبِيهِ عَنِ النَّبِيِّ ﷺ مُرْسَلًا، فَأَسْقَطَ أَبَا سَعِيدٍ، وَلَهُ طُرُقٌ يُقَوِّي بَعْضُهَا بَعْضًا.

It was related on the authority of Abū Saʿīd Saʿad bin Mālik bin Sinān al-Khudrī رضي الله عنه that the Messenger of Allāh صلى الله عليه وسلم said, «There should be neither harming nor reciprocating harm.»

A *ḥasan ḥadīth* which *Ibn Mājah, al-Dāraquṭnī*, and others related as having sound *isnād*. And Imam Mālik related in his *Muwaṭṭā'* with a broken *isnād*, from *'Amr bin Yaḥya*, from his father, from the

Prophet صَلَّى ٱللَّهُ عَلَيْهِ وَسَلَّمَ, but dropping (the name of) *Abū Sa'īd*. This *ḥadīth* has lines of transmission which strengthen one another (so that it may be regarded as having sound *isnād*).

Summarised Lessons

- Harming someone else in response to the harm that another has done is never to be a goal in itself. Justice and equity is a goal but not simply the harming of another. Therefore, for example, if A destroys B's property, then B does not have the right to go and destroy A's property. There is no benefit in that. There is only harm and waste of wealth in such an action. In this case, A is required to pay B for his losses. The ruling, though, is different in the case of bodily retribution or the Law of Retaliation. This is because, in general, no price can be put on such losses and one has the right to enact the same act upon the guilty party.
- In Islam, one should never cause any unjustifiable harm to others.
- Similarly, one should not respond to another's harm by causing him harm. He can demand his Sharī'ah rights but he cannot go beyond that to harm the other person further.

الحديث الثالث والثلاثون

Thirty-Third Ḥadīth

The Burden of Proof is on the Claimant

عَنِ ابْنِ عَبَّاسٍ رَضِيَ اللّٰهُ عَنْهُمَا أَنَّ رَسُولَ اللّٰهِ ﷺ قَالَ «لَوْ يُعْطَى النَّاسُ بِدَعْوَاهُمْ لَادَّعَى رِجَالٌ أَمْوَالَ قَوْمٍ وَدِمَاءَهُمْ، لكِنَّ الْبَيِّنَةَ عَلَى الْمُدَّعِي، وَالْيَمِينَ عَلَى مَنْ أَنْكَرَ.»

حَدِيثٌ حَسَنٌ، رَوَاهُ الْبَيْهَقِيّ في "السنن" [١٠/٢٥٢] وَغَيْرُهُ هَكَذَا، وَبَعْضُهُ فِي "الصَّحِيحَيْنِ."

Ibn ʿAbbās رَضِيَ ٱللَّهُ عَنْهُ said that the Messenger of Allāh صَلَّى ٱللَّهُ عَلَيْهِ وَسَلَّمَ said, «Were people to be given according to their claims, people would claim the wealth and blood of others. But the burden of proof is upon the claimant and the taking of an oath is upon the one who denies (the allegation).»

An excellent *ḥadīth* which *al-Bayhaqī*

and others have related. Parts of it are in the two *Ṣaḥīḥ* books.

Summarised Lessons

- Laws must be structured to prevent men from enforcing false claims against others. If the laws of evidence and procedure are not respected, people would start claiming everybody else's property and wealth.

- The burden of proof is upon the claimant. He is claiming something that goes against the apparent or obvious situation.

- If the claimant cannot provide any proof, the defendant may make an oath to clear himself of all charges or claims against him.

- Islam is a complete way of life. It contains correct beliefs, pure acts of worship, noble character, and a remarkable code of law. It gives everyone his due rights. It protects the wealth, life, and honour of the people. Since disputes and claims are a normal part of human life, Islam has enacted the proper and best means to bring an end to such disputes in a just manner. This *ḥadīth* is one example of how the Sharīʿah achieves such a lofty goal.

الحديث الرابع والثلاثون

Thirty-Fourth Ḥadīth

Enjoining Good and Forbidding Evil

عَنْ أَبِي سَعِيدٍ الْخُدْرِيِّ رَضِيَ اللهُ عَنْهُ قَالَ سَمِعْتُ رَسُولَ اللهِ ﷺ يَقُولُ «مَنْ رَأَى مِنْكُمْ مُنْكَرًا فَلْيُغَيِّرْهُ بِيَدِهِ، فَإِنْ لَمْ يَسْتَطِعْ فَبِلِسَانِهِ، فَإِنْ لَمْ يَسْتَطِعْ فَبِقَلْبِهِ، وَذَلِكَ أَضْعَفُ الْإِيمَانِ.»

رَوَاهُ مُسْلِمٌ [رقم ٤٩].

On the authority of Abū Sa'īd al-Khudrī رَضِيَ اللهُ عَنْهُ, who said, "I heard the Messenger of Allāh صَلَّى اللهُ عَلَيْهِ وَسَلَّمَ saying, «When any one of you sees anything that is disapproved (by Allāh), let him change it with his hand. If he is not able to do so, then let him change it with his tongue. And if he is not able to do so, then let him change it with his heart, and that is the weakest of faith.»"

Muslim.

Summarised Lessons

- A Muslim should never acquiesce to the presence of an evil. It is obligatory upon him to remove that evil whenever he has the ability to do so.
- If he can remove that evil with his hand, then he must do so.
- If he does not have the ability to remove the evil with his hand or if removing it would lead to a greater evil, then he must try to remove the evil with his speech.
- If he is also not able to remove the evil with his speech, then he can only resort to removing the evil with his heart. That is the least manifestation of faith with respect to evil.
- It is part of Allāh's mercy upon His servants that He does not hold them responsible for things which are beyond their ability or control.

الحديث الخامس والثلاثون

Thirty-Fifth Ḥadīth

Evil Acts that Ruin Brotherhood

عَنْ أَبِي هُرَيْرَةَ رَضِيَٱللَّهُعَنْهُ قَالَ: قَالَ رَسُولُ اللهِ صَلَّىٱللَّهُعَلَيْهِوَسَلَّمَ «لَا تَحَاسَدُوا، وَلَا تَنَاجَشُوا، وَلَا تَبَاغَضُوا، وَلَا تَدَابَرُوا، وَلَا يَبِعْ بَعْضُكُمْ عَلَى بَيْعِ بَعْضٍ، وَكُونُوا عِبَادَ اللهِ إِخْوَانًا، الْمُسْلِمُ أَخُو الْمُسْلِمِ، لَا يَظْلِمُهُ، وَلَا يَخْذُلُهُ، وَلَا يَكْذِبُهُ، وَلَا يَحْقِرُهُ، التَّقْوَى هَاهُنَا، وَيُشِيرُ إِلَى صَدْرِهِ ثَلَاثَ مَرَّاتٍ، بِحَسْبِ امْرِئٍ مِنَ الشَّرِّ أَنْ يَحْقِرَ أَخَاهُ الْمُسْلِمَ، كُلُّ الْمُسْلِمِ عَلَى الْمُسْلِمِ حَرَامٌ: دَمُهُ وَمَالُهُ وَعِرْضُهُ.»

رَوَاهُ مُسْلِمٌ [رقم ٢٥٦٤].

Abū Hurayrah رَضِيَٱللَّهُعَنْهُ reported that the Messenger of Allāh صَلَّىٱللَّهُعَلَيْهِوَسَلَّمَ said, «Do not be envious of one another, do not artificially inflate prices against one another, do not hate one another, do not shun one another, and do not undercut one another in business transactions, and be servants of Allāh as fellow-brothers. A Muslim is the brother of a Muslim. He does not oppress him, nor abandons him, nor lies to him, nor shows contempt for him. Piety is here – and he pointed to his chest three times. It is evil enough for a Muslim to hold his brother Muslim in contempt. All of a Muslim is inviolable to another Muslim: his blood, his property, and his honour.»

Muslim.

Summarised Lessons

- Muslims are all servants of Allāh and they must look at each other and actually treat each other like brothers. This brotherhood is not something that merely exists on the lips but it must actually be put into practice in everyday living.

- The true estimate of a person's worth is his *taqwā*. It is not the outer manifestations of this world, such as wealth, position, lineage, and so forth. But *taqwā* is in the heart and no one except Allāh knows the level of a person's *taqwā*. No Muslim can know for certain that he has more *taqwā* than another Muslim. Therefore, no Muslim could ever know for certain that he is better than another Muslim. Since that is the case, there is no call for a Muslim ever to look down upon or show contempt for his Muslim brother. Indeed, this is a great evil. In fact, that by itself is a sufficient amount of evil for anyone to carry.

- A Muslim is inviolable to every other Muslim. In other words, every Muslim must treat every other Muslim with the proper amount of respect and good behaviour.

- In particular, one must realize that a Muslim's blood is inviolable. One must avoid any illegal form of spilling of Muslim blood or physically injuring a Muslim.

- Similarly, a Muslim's wealth is also inviolable. One must respect the private property of his brother and should not use it unless it is known that his brother approves of that act.

- Finally, one must also show utmost respect for his brother's honour. He must be careful of his tongue and never wrongfully harm the honour of his brother.

الحديث السادس والثلاثون

Thirty-Sixth Ḥadīth

Fulfilling the needs of a Muslim and the Blessings of Seeking Knowledge

عَنْ أَبِي هُرَيْرَةَ رَضِيَ اللَّهُ عَنْهُ عَنِ النَّبِيِّ ﷺ قَالَ «مَنْ نَفَّسَ عَنْ مُؤْمِنٍ كُرْبَةً مِنْ كُرَبِ الدُّنْيَا نَفَّسَ اللهُ عَنْهُ كُرْبَةً مِنْ كُرَبِ يَوْمِ الْقِيَامَةِ، وَمَنْ يَسَّرَ عَلَى مُعْسِرٍ، يَسَّرَ اللهُ عَلَيْهِ فِي الدُّنْيَا وَالْآخِرَةِ، وَمَنْ سَتَرَ مُسْلِمًا سَتَرَهُ اللهُ فِي الدُّنْيَا وَالْآخِرَةِ، وَاللهُ فِي عَوْنِ الْعَبْدِ مَا كَانَ الْعَبْدُ فِي عَوْنِ أَخِيهِ، وَمَنْ سَلَكَ طَرِيقًا يَلْتَمِسُ فِيهِ عِلْمًا سَهَّلَ اللهُ لَهُ بِهِ طَرِيقًا إِلَى الْجَنَّةِ، وَمَا اجْتَمَعَ قَوْمٌ فِي بَيْتٍ مِنْ بُيُوتِ اللهِ يَتْلُونَ كِتَابَ اللهِ، وَيَتَدَارَسُونَهُ فِيمَا بَيْنَهُمْ؛ إِلَّا نَزَلَتْ عَلَيْهِمُ السَّكِينَةُ،

وَغَشِيَتْهُمُ الرَّحْمَةُ، وَذَكَرَهُمُ اللهُ فِيمَنْ عِنْدَهُ، وَمَنْ أَبْطَأَ بِهِ عَمَلُهُ لَمْ يُسْرِعْ بِهِ نَسَبُهُ.»

رَوَاهُ مُسْلِمٌ [رقم ٢٦٩٩] بهذا اللفظ.

It was related on the authority of Abū Hurayrah رَضِيَ اللَّهُ عَنْهُ that the Prophet صَلَّى اللَّهُ عَلَيْهِ وَسَلَّمَ said, «Whosoever relieves from a believer some grief pertaining to this world, Allāh will relieve from him some grief pertaining to the Hereafter. Whosoever alleviates the difficulties of a needy person who cannot pay his debt, Allāh will alleviate his difficulties in both this world and the Hereafter. Whosoever conceals the faults of a Muslim, Allah will conceal his faults in this world and the Hereafter. Allāh will aid a servant (of His) so long as the servant aids his brother. Whosoever follows a path to seek knowledge therein, Allāh will make easy for him a path to Paradise. No people gather together in one of the houses of Allāh, reciting the Book of Allāh and studying it among themselves, except that tranquillity descends upon them, mercy covers them, the angels surround them, and Allāh makes mention of them amongst those who are in His presence. Whosoever is slowed down by his deeds will not be hastened forward by his lineage.»

Muslim.

Summarised Lessons

- The reward for deeds is of the same nature as the deeds themselves. Therefore, if a Muslim relieves his brother of some distress, Allāh will relieve him of some greater distress in the Hereafter. If a person alleviates a person's debt, Allāh will alleviate a difficult situation for him. If a person conceals his brothers' sins, Allāh will conceal his sins. Indeed, if a Muslim is helping his brother in any way, then Allāh will be helping him as long as he is helping his brother.

- The path to Paradise is made easy by seeking knowledge. Through knowledge one can recognize that path and can have the qualities in the heart that will lead him to follow that path.

- Gathering together to read and study the Quran is one of the most important means of attaining knowledge. It is a deed that is very pleasing to Allāh and has many resultant benefits associated with it.

- If a person's deeds are not sufficient to earn him entrance into Paradise, his lineage, no matter how noble, will not be able to assist him in any way.

- The example of coming together, reciting, learning, and studying the Quran was set by the noblest of messengers and the noblest of angels. Al-Bukhārī and Muslim record that Prophet Muḥammad ﷺ and the Angel Gabriel would meet every Ramaḍān to go over and recite the Quran. In the last year of the Prophet's life, they went over the Quran twice.

الحديث السابع والثلاثون

Thirty-Seventh Ḥadīth

The Recording of Deeds

عَنْ ابْنِ عَبَّاسٍ رَضِيَ اللَّهُ عَنْهُمَا عَنْ رَسُولِ اللَّهِ ﷺ فِيمَا يَرْوِيهِ عَنْ رَبِّهِ تَبَارَكَ وَتَعَالَى، قَالَ: «إِنَّ اللَّهَ كَتَبَ الْحَسَنَاتِ وَالسَّيِّئَاتِ، ثُمَّ بَيَّنَ ذَلِكَ، فَمَنْ هَمَّ بِحَسَنَةٍ فَلَمْ يَعْمَلْهَا كَتَبَهَا اللَّهُ عِنْدَهُ حَسَنَةً كَامِلَةً، وَإِنْ هَمَّ بِهَا فَعَمِلَهَا كَتَبَهَا اللَّهُ عِنْدَهُ عَشْرَ حَسَنَاتٍ إِلَى سَبْعِمِائَةِ ضِعْفٍ إِلَى أَضْعَافٍ كَثِيرَةٍ، وَإِنْ هَمَّ بِسَيِّئَةٍ فَلَمْ يَعْمَلْهَا كَتَبَهَا اللَّهُ عِنْدَهُ حَسَنَةً كَامِلَةً، وَإِنْ هَمَّ بِهَا فَعَمِلَهَا كَتَبَهَا اللَّهُ سَيِّئَةً وَاحِدَةً.»

رَوَاهُ الْبُخَارِيُّ [رقم ٦٤٩١] وَمُسْلِمٌ [رقم ١٣١] في "صحيحيهما" بهذه الحروف.

Ibn ʿAbbās رَضِيَ اللَّهُ عَنْهُمَا reported that the Messenger of Allāh صَلَّى اللَّهُ عَلَيْهِ وَسَلَّمَ related from his Lord سُبْحَانَهُ وَتَعَالَى, «Verily Allāh has recorded the good deeds and the evil deeds.» Then he clarified that, «Whosoever intends to do a good deed but does not do it, Allāh records it with Himself as a complete good deed; but if he intends it and does it, Allāh records it with Himself as ten good deeds, up to seven hundred times, or more than that. But if he intends to do an evil deed and does not do it, Allāh records it with Himself as a complete good deed; but if he intends it and does it, Allāh records it down as one evil deed.»

Al-Bukhārī and *Muslim*.

Summarised Lessons

- This is another *ḥadīth*, like Ḥadīth 1 in this collection, that demonstrates the importance of having a good intention. A person will have recorded for himself good deeds simply because of his intention. Hence, once again, his good intentions can take him beyond what his actual deeds might be.
- Allāh has decreed what the good deeds and evil deeds are. He has recorded the deeds of mankind or has ordered the angels to record the deeds of mankind in the manner described in this *ḥadīth*.

- First, if a person truly decides to do a good deed and then ends up not doing it, Allāh will have recorded for him one good deed.
- Second, if the person actually performs the good deed, it will be multiplied for him by a multiple of ten up to a multiple of whatever Allāh, in His mercy and grace, wills.
- Third, if a person decides to do an evil deed and then, for the sake of Allāh, he changes his way and does not do that deed, Allāh will record for him one good deed.
- Fourth, if a person actually does perform the evil deed, Allāh will only record one evil deed against him.
- Such is the mercy and grace of Allāh. With this type of reckoning, only those who truly deserve to be destroyed and punished will be destroyed and punished.

الحديث الثامن والثلاثون

Thirty-Eighth Ḥadīth

The Concept of *Wilāyah*

عَنْ أَبِي هُرَيْرَة رَضِيَ اللهُ عَنْهُ قَالَ: قَالَ رَسُول اللهِ ﷺ «إِنَّ اللهَ تَعَالَى قَالَ: [مَنْ عَادَى لِي وَلِيًّا فَقَدْ آذَنْتهُ بِالْحَرْبِ، وَمَا تَقَرَّبَ إلَيَّ عَبْدِي بِشَيْءٍ أَحَبَّ إلَيَّ مِمَّا افْتَرَضْتُهُ عَلَيْهِ، وَلَا يَزَالُ عَبْدِي يَتَقَرَّبُ إلَيَّ بِالنَّوَافِلِ حَتَّى أُحِبَّهُ، فَإِذَا أَحْبَبْتُهُ كُنْت سَمْعَهُ الَّذِي يَسْمَعُ بِهِ، وَبَصَرَهُ الَّذِي يُبْصِرُ بِهِ، وَيَدَهُ الَّتِي يَبْطِشُ بِهَا، وَرِجْلَهُ الَّتِي يَمْشِي بِهَا، وَلَئِنْ سَأَلَنِي لَأُعْطِيَنَّهُ، وَلَئِنْ اسْتَعَاذَنِي لَأُعِيذَنَّهُ.]»

رَوَاهُ الْبُخَارِيُّ [رقم ٦٥٠٢].

Abū Hurayrah رَضِيَ اللهُ عَنْهُ reported that the Messenger of Allāh صَلَّى اللهُ عَلَيْهِ وَسَلَّمَ said, «Allāh has said, "Whosoever acts with enmity towards a *walī* of Mine, I will indeed declare war against him. Nothing endears My servant to Me more than doing what I have made obligatory upon him. And My servant continues to draw nearer to Me with supererogatory prayers so that I love him. When I love him, I shall be his hearing with which he hears, his sight with which he sees, his hands with which he holds, and his feet with which he walks. And were he to ask (something) of Me, I would surely give it to him, and if he takes refuge in Me, I would certainly grant him it."»

Al-Bukhārī.

Summarised Lessons

- To oppose one of Allāh's devotees is equivalent to opposing or fighting Allāh.
- This *ḥadīth* demonstrates the *power* of the beloved slaves of Allāh. Such slaves are never left on their own but instead they have the full support and aid of Allāh, the All-Powerful.
- There is nothing equal to the obligatory deeds.
- Obligatory acts are the most beloved to Allāh and one should perform them first and then move on to the voluntary deeds, and not vice-versa.

- The one who performs the obligatory and voluntary deeds moves closest to Allāh.
- Allāh blesses His beloved servants with special guidance and mercy as well as answering their prayers.
- Whatever level a slave reaches, he must always keep his relationship with Allāh in complete submission. When he is in need, he must turn to Allāh. When he seeks refuge, he must seek refuge in Allāh. Due to his close relationship with Allāh, Allāh will respond quickly to him under those circumstances.

الحديث التاسع والثلاثون

Thirty-Ninth Ḥadīth

The Pardoned Actions

عَنِ ابْنِ عَبَّاسٍ رَضِيَ اللهُ عَنْهُمَا أَنَّ رَسُولَ اللهِ ﷺ قَالَ «إِنَّ اللهَ تَجَاوَزَ لِي عَنْ أُمَّتِي الْخَطَأَ وَالنِّسْيَانَ وَمَا اسْتُكْرِهُوا عَلَيْهِ.»

حَدِيثٌ حَسَنٌ، رَوَاهُ ابْنُ مَاجَهْ [رقم ٢٠٤٥] وَالْبَيْهَقِيِّ في "السنن" [رقم ٧].

Ibn ʿAbbās رَضِيَ اللَّهُ عَنْهُ reported that the Messenger of Allāh صَلَّى اللَّهُ عَلَيْهِ وَسَلَّمَ said, «Truly Allāh has for my sake pardoned the mistakes and forgetfulness of my community, and for what they have done under force or duress.»

A fine *ḥadīth* related by *Ibn Mājah, al-Bayhaqī,* and others.

Summarised Lessons

- This *ḥadīth* is extremely important to the topic of personal responsibility. In the way that it is understood by some, it has ramifications for virtually every area of *fiqh*. It demonstrates that Allāh does not consider people sinful when their actions are not representative of their intentions. In general, a sin is something done against the Sharīʿah, knowingly and willingly.

- By Allāh's mercy, He has decreed that He will overlook for Prophet Muḥammad's ﷺ followers what they do by mistake, out of forgetfulness, or due to coercion.

- This means that Allāh forgives any sinful aspect of those deeds but it does not mean that the worldly rulings concerning those deeds are to be overlooked.

الحديث الأربعون

Fortieth Ḥadīth

This World is Temporary

عَنِ ابْنِ عُمَرَ رَضِيَ اللهُ عَنْهُمَا قَالَ: أَخَذَ رَسُولُ اللهِ ﷺ بِمَنْكِبِي، وَقَالَ «كُنْ فِي الدُّنْيَا كَأَنَّكَ غَرِيبٌ أَوْ عَابِرُ سَبِيلٍ.» وَكَانَ ابْنُ عُمَرَ رَضِيَ اللهُ عَنْهُمَا يَقُولُ: إِذَا أَمْسَيْتَ فَلَا تَنْتَظِرِ الصَّبَاحَ، وَإِذَا أَصْبَحْتَ فَلَا تَنْتَظِرِ الْمَسَاءَ، وَخُذْ مِنْ صِحَّتِكَ لِمَرَضِكَ، وَمِنْ حَيَاتِكَ لِمَوْتِكَ.

رَوَاهُ الْبُخَارِيُّ [رقم ٦٤١٦].

On the authority of Ibn ʿUmar رَضِيَ اللهُ عَنْهُمَا who said, "The Messenger of Allāh صَلَّى اللهُ عَلَيْهِ وَسَلَّمَ took me by the shoulder and said, «Be in this world as though you were a stranger or a traveler along a path.»"

Ibn ʿUmar رَضِيَ اللهُ عَنْهُمَا used to say, "When evening comes, do not expect (to live till) morning, and when morning comes, do not expect (to live till) evening. Take from your health for your illness and from your life for your death."

Al-Bukhārī.

Summarised Lessons

- A believer has one of two attitudes toward this worldly life: that of a stranger or that of a traveler along a path. His heart and his sights must be set on his real home and final resting place.
- The believer takes from this world the provisions that he needs to reach his final destination. He must always prepare for death and not expect to be living in this world forever.
- The believer takes advantage of those resources or opportunities that Allāh has given him before it is too late. He takes advantage of his health before sickness comes to him and his life before death comes to him.
- Paradise for the believer is like—nay, greater than—the joy a traveler feels when he finally reaches his destination and the joy that a person feels when he is finally in the company of those with whom he belongs, in the place where he belongs.

- In this *ḥadīth*, the Prophet ﷺ has instructed Muslims to give this world and this life its proper due, all toward the overall goal of achieving the good of the Hereafter. In other words, even the stranger and the traveler have to meet their needs in this world. They make sure that they meet these needs in such a way that it does not harm their overall goal. Hence, this *ḥadīth* is not implying that one must abandon everything of this world. Instead, it is implying that one's heart should not be attached to this world (like a stranger), and that one is only taking from this world what he needs to carry on his journey to his destination (like a traveler).

الحديث الحادي والأربعون

Forty-First Ḥadīth

Inclination towards Revelation

عَنْ أَبِي مُحَمَّدٍ عَبْدِ اللهِ بْنِ عَمْرِو بْنِ الْعَاصِ رَضِيَ اللهُ عَنْهُمَا قَالَ: قَالَ رَسُولُ اللهِ ﷺ «لَا يُؤْمِنُ أَحَدُكُمْ حَتَّى يَكُونَ هَوَاهُ تَبَعًا لِمَا جِئْتُ بِهِ.»

حَدِيثٌ حَسَنٌ صَحِيحٌ، رَوَيْنَاهُ فِي كِتَابِ "الْحُجَّةِ" بِإِسْنَادٍ صَحِيحٍ.

Abū Muḥammad ʿAbdullāh bin ʿAmr bin al-ʿĀṣ رَضِيَ اللَّهُ عَنْهُمَا reported that the Messenger of Allāh صَلَّى اللَّهُ عَلَيْهِ وَسَلَّمَ said, «None of you (truly) believes until his desire or inclination is in accordance with what I have brought or subservient to what I came with.»

A fine and genuine *ḥadīth* which was related in the book, *al-Ḥujjah*, with a *ṣaḥīḥ isnād*.

Summarised Lessons

- It is concluded that this *ḥadīth* is weak. Although there is no problem with the meaning of the *ḥadīth*, there is no call for anyone to quote it as a statement of the Prophet صَلَّى ٱللَّٰهُ عَلَيْهِ وَسَلَّمَ. There are sufficient other authentic and acceptable evidences to prove the same point that this *ḥadīth* states.

- Indeed, the meaning it expresses may be proven through numerous other authentic evidences. For example, Allāh says in the Quran, ﴿It is not for a believer, man or woman, when Allāh and His Messenger have decreed a matter that they should have any option in their decision. And whoever disobeys Allāh and His Messenger, he has indeed strayed into a plain error﴾ (al-Aḥzāb: 36) and ﴿But no, by your Lord, they have no faith until they make you [O Muḥammad] judge in all disputes between them, and find in themselves no resistance against your decisions and they submit to them with a full submission.﴾ (al-Nisāʾ: 65).

الحديث الثاني والأربعون

Forty-Second Ḥadīth

Seeking Allāh's Forgiveness

عَنْ أَنَسِ بْنِ مَالِكٍ رَضِيَ اللَّهُ عَنْهُ قَالَ: سَمِعْتُ رَسُولَ اللهِ ﷺ يَقُولُ «قَالَ اللهُ تَعَالَى [يَا ابْنَ آدَمَ! إِنَّكَ مَا دَعَوْتَنِي وَرَجَوْتَنِي غَفَرْتُ لَكَ عَلَى مَا كَانَ مِنْكَ وَلَا أُبَالِي، يَا ابْنَ آدَمَ! لَوْ بَلَغَتْ ذُنُوبُكَ عَنَانَ السَّمَاءِ ثُمَّ اسْتَغْفَرْتَنِي غَفَرْتُ لَكَ، يَا ابْنَ آدَمَ! إِنَّكَ لَوْ أَتَيْتَنِي بِقُرَابِ الْأَرْضِ خَطَايَا ثُمَّ لَقِيتَنِي لَا تُشْرِكُ بِي شَيْئًا لَأَتَيْتُكَ بِقُرَابِهَا مَغْفِرَةً].»

رَوَاهُ التِّرْمِذِيُّ [رقم ٣٥٤٠] وَقَالَ: حَدِيثٌ حَسَنٌ صَحِيحٌ.

From Anas رَضِيَ اللَّهُ عَنْهُ who said, "I heard the Messenger of Allāh صَلَّى اللَّهُ عَلَيْهِ وَسَلَّمَ say, «Allāh has said, 'O son of Ādam, so long as you call upon Me, and hope in Me, I shall forgive you for what you have done, and I shall not mind. O son of Ādam, were your sins to reach the clouds in the sky and were you then to ask forgiveness of Me, I shall forgive you. O son of Ādam, were you to come to Me with an earthful of sins and were you then to face Me, without having associated anything with Me, I shall grant you an earthful of forgiveness.'»"

Recorded by *al-Tirmidhī*, who said that it is a good and sound *ḥadīth*.

Summarised Lessons

- The means or causes of forgiveness are three: (1) Supplicating to Allāh with hope in Him; (2) Asking Allāh for forgiveness and repenting to Him; and (3) adhering to Tawḥīd (Islamic monotheism).
- No matter how great or how many a believer's sins, Allāh's forgiveness and mercy are greater and can encompass them all.
- The act of forgiving on Allāh's part does not harm Allāh in any way. Hence, one should earnestly seek His forgiveness and mercy.
- The forgiveness and clemency of Allāh are greater and more expansive than the sins believers commit.

- No one should ever feel despair for any sin he has committed—even the sin of Shirk (ascribing partners to Allāh) for years of one's life is removed by the embracing of Islam and repentance. So, the door to repentance is always open until the time of one's death. However, the repentance must be true and sincere.

- The believer should always be repentant and seek Allāh's forgiveness as he recognizes that his sins and mistakes toward Allāh are great and numerous.